Gateway to Teaching
From Pre-service to In-service

B. J. Enz and S. J. Cook

KENDALL/HUNT PUBLISHING COMPANY
2460 Kerper Boulevard P.O. Box 539 Dubuque, Iowa 52004-0539

Acknowledgments

The authors wish to thank the following individuals for their time, suggestions, critique, and support.

John Bennett	Nancy Moffat
MaryJo Carpenter	Geri Seton
Donald Freeman	Alice Shepard
Pam Gissell	Gloria Smith
Sandy Golner	Jill Stamm
Karen Kimerer	Elaine Stover
Roger Maresh	

A special thank you to Donald L. Enz, veteran high school teacher and administrator, for his contributions to the principal's principles and suggestions for secondary teachers.

The authors wish to thank:

Sharad Prabhu and Ravi Venkatasubramanian for their help with text preparation.

Carla Bruce for her expertise with textbook design and layout.

Chrys Gakopoulos and Brenda Braun for their marvelous illustrations.

About The Authors

Billie J. Enz is the Director of the Office of Professional Field Experiences in the College of Education at Arizona State University. In this position she has supervised the placement of approximately 1000 interns and student teachers each semester. She has also served as co-director for the ASU/Maricopa County Teacher Residency Training and Research Project, an induction program for beginning teachers. As a teacher and university instructor for twenty years, her interests currently focus on emergent literacy, play as learning in early childhood education, the social and pedagogical development of beginning teachers, and the effects of mentoring on veteran teachers.

Susan J. Cook is an Assistant Professor in educational Administration at Arizona State University West. In directing the field experience component of the teacher preparation program, she has placed and supervised pre-service education students in over 175 schools. As a teacher and administrator for seventeen years, her interests focused on early childhood education, teachers as curriculum developers, and site-based staff development. Currently, she is committed to the successful integration of university course-work with the field experiences provided for pre-service teachers in teacher education programs.

Contents

Introduction iv

1. **Marketing Yourself** 1

   Section A: 3
   The Typical Application Process—Becoming an Official Job Applicant
   Step 1: Creating a University Career Placement File
   Step 2: Official Job Application
   Step 3: District-Level "Paper" Screening
   Step 4: District-Level Initial Screening Interview
   Step 5: Principal's Selection Interview

   Section B: 28
   First Impressions: The Power of Presence
   Demeanor and Mannerisms: The Power of Communication

   References

2. **Putting It Together for the First Time** 33

   Section A: 36
   Management of Time and Task
   Determining, Teaching, and Reinforcing Routine Tasks
   Teaching Routines
   Task Analysis
   Lightening the Load: Student Helpers

   Section B: 46
   The Paper Avalanche

   Section C: 52
   Preparing for School: Mental Check Lists

   Section D: 57
   Designing a Lesson Plan Book
   The Long Haul to the Here and Now: Realities of Lesson Planning
   Thematic Units
   Lesson Plan Evaluation: Time for Reflection

   References

3. **Public Relations and the Beginning Teacher** 75

   Section A: 77
   First Day Communication
   Open House

   Section B: 87
   Newsletters/News Flashes/Phone Calls

     Section C: 95
        Parent Teacher Conferences
        Conference Scheduling
        Portfolio Evaluation System
        Observations and Anecdotal Notes
        Parent Conference Format and Forms
        Avoiding Conference Confrontations
        Managing Conference Confrontations
        Setting the Scene
    References

4. **The Law and the Public School Teacher** 111
        Pay Attention to Your Legal "Do's"

5. **The "Magic" of Student Management** 115
     Section A: 117
        Matching Philosophies
        Packaged Discipline Plans
        Age-Appropriate Techniques

     Section B: 123
        Parent Involvement
        Believe in the Magic: Teachers Talking to Teachers

6. **Juggling, Balancing, and Spinning . . . . Or Ways to Manage Stress** . . . 127
        Stress and the Beginning Teacher
        Creating a Comfortable Work Environment
        Recognizing and Relieving Stress
        Ways to Manage Stress
        Balance

7. **Yes, You Will Get Sick: Preparing for the Substitute Teacher** 135
     Section A: 137
        How to Make a Substitute Teacher Happy

     Section B: 142
        How to be a Successful Substitute Teacher
        Surviving as a Substitute
        Learning While You Substitute
    References

8. **Teaching in Culturally and Linguistically Diverse Classrooms** 147
   and Communities

        by Christian Faltis

   Section A: 149

      Expect to have English learners in your classroom

      What kinds of special instructional programs have English learners
      had before they entered your classroom?

         Transitional Bilingual Education

         Self-contained Immersion Programs

         Sheltered English Programs

         Pull-out English ESL Programs

      Who is eligible for bilingual education?

      How is language proficiency assessed?

         Language Assessment Scale

      Caution: A word about labels

   Section B: 155

      What can we do to help ESL students join in our classroom?

   Section C: 158

      What about involving parents who don't speak English?

9. **Working with Special Needs Children in the Regular** 163
   Classroom Mainstream

        by Samuel A. DiGangi

   Section A: 166

      Least Restrictive Environment

   Section B: 171

      Limitations of Categorical Labels

   Section C: 174

      Questions about Teaching Special Education Students

   Section D: 180

      Collaboration/Consultation

   Section E: 182

      The IEP

   Section F: 186

      Physical Handicaps

   References

10. **Tips from a Veteran First Year Teacher** 197

Gateway to Teaching: From Pre-service to In-service

Bridging the gap from student teacher to teacher-in-the-classroom is a challenging transition. *Gateway to Teaching: From Pre-service to In-service* is designed to provide practical and timely information to the beginning teacher, regardless of the grade level or content area to which novices are assigned.

Beyond the theory is the practice, and the topics presented in this text are based on four years of research on beginning teachers' needs during the student teaching experience through the first induction year. In addition, the authors surveyed and interviewed scores of veteran teachers who worked as mentors to student and beginning teachers. This information confirmed and added depth to our findings; the resulting information is presented in this text.

The content includes "Marketing Yourself," information about how to obtain the first professional teaching position, to "Juggling, Balancing, and Spinning," a chapter that deals with beginning teacher stress. *Gateway* includes specific content, sample forms, and illustrative examples that novice teachers may use in developing management and organization plans for their own classrooms. The text features information that is useful to all beginning teachers. When appropriate, specific content information is presented by level, for example, primary, intermediate, and secondary. Thus, the text is highly appropriate as a foundation for developing and presenting student teaching seminars and induction or mentoring programs with beginning teachers.

Chapter 1

Marketing Yourself

Section A:
The Typical Application Process — An Overview
Becoming an Official Job Applicant

Step 1: Creating A University Career Placement File

Step 2: Official Job Application

Guide to Writing Resumes

References/Recommendations

Step 3: District-Level "Paper" Screening

Step 4: District-Level Initial Screening Interview

Step 5: Principal's Selection Interview

Developing and Using A Portfolio

Section B:
First Impressions: The Power of Presence

Demeanor and Mannerisms:
The Power of Communication

References

Section A

The Typical Application Process

Obtaining your first professional position is always an exciting challenge. The purpose of this chapter is to review a typical application/interview process that most districts use when searching for the "person best suited for the job." In addition, this chapter will discuss some techniques that highlight your unique talents and skills. Further, we'll review the power of the first impression and provide research-based suggestions that will enable you to use those first moments in an interview to your best advantage.

Typical Application/Interview Process

Step 1: Creating A University Career Placement File

You:
- Accurately and neatly complete forms at the University Career Placement Center

Step 2: Official Job Applications

You:
- Develop resume/philosophy of education statement
- Accurately, neatly, and completely fill out official district job application form
- Send University Career Placement File to district
- Send Official University Transcripts to district

Step 3: District-Level "Paper" Screening

They:
- Review all potential teacher applications
- Form a pool of qualified applicants
- Check your references
- Contact you, if you are selected to proceed in the application process

Step 4: District-Level Initial Screening Interview

You:
- Make best first impression (portfolio optional)

They:
- Conduct structured interview
- Evaluate your responses and professional demeanor
- Identify best potential hires — those that are most qualified and those that made strongest professional presentation

Step 5: Principal's Selection Interview

They:
- Look for a best "fit" — enthusiastic, dedicated
- Conduct formal and informal interviews

You:
- Use portfolio to reveal strengths, experience, and personality — "Will I fit?"

Step 1. Creating A University Career Service File

Almost all colleges and universities have a Career Center. Most of these centers have specific forms and materials they wish you to complete. These forms often include:

General information page (name, address, phone, and major)

Course and grade report

References

Districts will always require that you send them your University Career File. You, in turn, may request that the Career Service Office send your "official" file to the districts to whom you have applied.

Career Services are a wonderful resource for potential teachers. They may provide a range of services, including resume development workshops, seminars on interviewing techniques, and organizing screening interviews with potential employers.

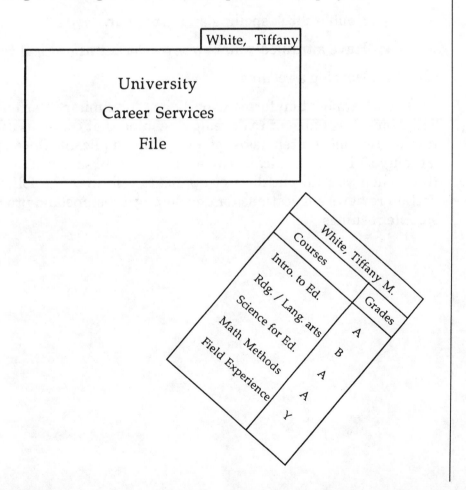

Step 2: Official Job Applications

Paper screening includes the process in which districts generally catalog applicant files by grade level(s) or subject areas. When a particular position becomes available, personnel staff simply refer to the appropriate files. Frequently, large metropolitan districts report that they will have 200-300 qualified applicants for one position. With that many applications to consider, district personnel directors are looking for reasons to exclude files. Your application forms are the district's first impression of you. Many decisions are made about the type of person you are based only on the quality and appearance of your application forms. You may be the best applicant for the position, but unless your personnel file represents you well, you will not be considered.

Therefore, personnel directors recommend the following:

- ✔ All forms should be completely and neatly filled out.
- ✔ Applications should be legible.
- ✔ Double check spelling and grammar.
- ✔ Have a trained editor review your forms.
- ✔ Develop a resume.

District application forms usually ask for similar information. Therefore, it is efficient to develop a resume that compiles all the information most often asked of a teaching applicant. Developing a thoughtful, grammatically correct resume will save you hours of time when you fill out district application forms. The following section reviews suggestions for developing a resume and provides sample resumes.

Guide to Writing Resumes

Education — list your most current degree first, then your GPA.

Certificates — list all certificates and endorsements you have earned (Early Childhood, ESL/BLE, etc.)

Experience — list the most recent teaching experience first — which, for novices, is student teaching.

Related Experience/Community Service — again, the most recent is listed first. Keep in mind that the prospective employer wants a person that has demonstrated he/she can work effectively with students. Therefore, any experience/service you list should be related to the teaching position you are seeking. If possible, describe the major emphasis of the position with action words, for exmple, taught, coached, directed, counseled, tested, evaluated.

> ✔ Younger, less experienced applicants may wish to identify college or high school accomplishments.

Special Talents/Attributes — list those activities that highlight your teaching ability, scholarship, communication skills, or artistic/athletic talents that illustrate the unique contributions you could make to the school/district.

Honors — employers wish to hire individuals who are dedicated and excel. List any type of honor you have received.

References — list people who have actually observed your teaching ability, including, your cooperating teacher, college supervisor, department or grade level chair, and/or building administrators. It is very important that you list your references' contact information carefully. Home phone numbers are necessary since most hiring is completed during the summer. Include a list of references on your resume and on your University Career Placement File.

Resume — Example for Elementary Candidates

Sally Smith, 6266 N. North, Anytown, AZ. 85666 (xxx-xxx-xxxx)

EDUCATION:

1992 — Bachelor of Arts in Education, Arizona State University
Grade Point Average 3.46

CERTIFICATES:

Elementary Education
Early Childhood Endorsement

EXPERIENCE:

Fall 1992 — Student Teaching, Best Elementary, Any District, Anytown, Arizona. Second Grade.

RELATED EXPERIENCE/COMMUNITY SERVICE:

1988-89 Swim Instructor, Anytown Community Recreation Center

- Designed and implemented beginner's swim program.
- Instructed 5–6–and 7–year old's beginning swimming classes.
- Directed "Swim Night" for parents.

1989-90 Arts/Crafts Instructor, Anytown Parks & Recreation

- Planned and taught arts & crafts to 3–4– and 5–year olds.
- Compiled projects and hosted an Open House for families.

HONORS:

- Dean's Honor Roll

ATTRIBUTES:

One semester of student teaching, three semesters of internship and work experiences listed above have provided an excellent start in my teaching career. My classroom strengths lie in the following areas:

- Rapport and communication with students and parents.
- Professional and positive attitude.
- Planning and classroom management skill.
- Enthusiasm, motivation, and energy.
- Dependability and good judgment.

REFERENCES:

Mrs. Sarah Perfect (Cooperating Teacher, Second Grade) Best Elementary, Any District, Anytown, Arizona.

School Address	School Phone
Home Address	Home Phone

Dr. Kelly Great, Principal, Best Elementary, Any District, Anytown, Arizona.

School Address	School Phone
Home Address	Home Phone

Dr. C. Terrific, College Supervisor, Arizona State University, Tempe, Arizona.

University Address	University Phone
Home Address	Home Phone

Resume — Example for Secondary Candidates

PERSONAL BACKGROUND:

Raul Gomez, 2020 West Broadway, Everytown, Arizona 85333 (xxx-xxx-xxxx)

EDUCATION:

Arizona State University: Post-Baccalaureate Certification and Master of Education programs in Secondary Education (1980-90). G.P.A. 3.86.

Southern Alabama University: (1972—1974) Doctoral work in Sociology.

University of Ohio: MA (8/72) in Sociology.

University of Ohio: Bachelor of Science (5/71) in Sociology (Political Science).

CERTIFICATES:

Secondary Education—Social Sciences

TEACHING EXPERIENCE:

Wonderful County Community College District: Part-time Instructor for Sociology, Political Science.

Happy Valley School Districts: Substitute in Social Studies and English (Fall, 1989).
Student teacher in Social Studies, Happy HS (Sp '90)

American Federation Employees: Education Coordinator (1983-84).

Tulsa Area Technical College: Part-time Sociology Instructor (Fall '82).

University of Minnesota: Sociology Instructor (Fall '76).

University of Minnesota: Chair and Sociology Instructor, (1974-76). President, University Collegium. Assistant Coach for Women's Athletics.

RELATED

Commission on the Arizona Environment: Assistant to the Director (1986-88). Wrote environmental reports, helped plan/coordinate state-wide conferences and special projects, and provided environmental education programs to public schools.

Arizona Veterans Service Commission: Veterans Service Officer (1984-85).

COMMUNITY ACTIVITIES

World Affairs Council of Arizona: Served as host and consultant to international guests selected for their present/future leadership roles in their countries, and on the Board of Directors. Chair, *Great Decisions* program.

Other activities include *Arizona Political Collectors,* and the *Committee for the Bicentennial of the French Revolution, Alliance Francaise..*

ACADEMIC HONORS

Alpha Kappa Delta, International Sociology Honor Society, Phi Kappa Phi, National Honor Society.

References/Recommendations

The purpose of a reference is to validate that you can do the job. Whether it is an oral reference (telephone, personal conversation) or written, the process is the same.

Your recommendations and references are critical to your success as a serious job contender. Anything you can do to help the reference writer become more familiar with specific information about you will ultimately work to your benefit. Therefore, it is extremely helpful if you supply the reference writer with your resume and also provide details about the position you are seeking. This additional information will greatly help the reference writer compose a strong recommendation.

A complete set of recommendations should include the following.

1. References should include the identity of the referent, position held, and explain the context or situations in which the referent has interacted with the candidate.

2. The referent should identify and elaborate specific personal and professional strengths that the candidate possesses.

3. Finally, the referent should remark on the candidate's professional potential.

Example of a strong recommendation:

Our school serves a predominately minority at-risk population in a large urban district. John Mr. Perfect taught in a self-contained second grade classroom. He has been a superior role model for learning. He demonstrated this to the students through his enthusiasm and positive attitude that education is important. John is very dependable and a conscientious student teacher. He consistently displayed a professional attitude and worked towards being more self-confident in using the assertive discipline plan and was effectively maintaining positive classroom behavior by the close of the semester. Mr. Perfect demonstrates a genuine eagerness to improve in all aspects of his teaching style. He shows this desire to improve his teaching by asking and seeking new and better techniques. I highly recommend him for any teaching position. I feel he will develop into a valuable member of any faculty in which he might be placed.

Step 3: District-Level "Paper" Screening

District Application Procedures

To become an applicant most districts require you to:

- File a complete official district application form with the District Personnel Department. All information requested on the application form should be filled out accurately and completely. Even if you have a professional resume developed, responding "See resume" will not suffice for any information requested. Please be specific as to subject/grade level(s) preferences(s).

- Submit a copy of all up-to-date transcripts of college/university credits or request the registrar of your university to send it to the district.

- Request that a copy of your current University Career Placement File be sent to their offices. The University Career Placement File should contain at least three letters of recommendation in addition to your final Student Teaching Evaluation.

These documents constitute the application file. Only after all these forms are completed and are in the district personnel office can you be considered an active applicant. At this point, the district begins to conduct a "paper screening."

The following pages include Example A, a typical application form, and Example B, a questionnaire supplement that a district might ask you to complete. These questions may also be used in an interview.

Example A: Large Public School District

ALL TOWN PUBLIC SCHOOLS

The application for employment is a legal document.
Any information you provide must be accurate.

APPLICATION FOR
CERTIFICATED EMPLOYMENT

Dr.
Mr.
Mrs. _____
Miss   LAST   FIRST   MIDDLE
Ms.

Date _____

Position Desired (*First Preference Only*) _____
                                     GRADE LEVEL AND/OR SUBJECT

IMPORTANT: Before final consideration for employment, the candidate must have on file in the personnel office a complete set of transcripts and a placement file. It is a candidate's responsiblity to see that transcripts and placement files are provided. A screening interview is also required. Out-of-state candidates should write to the State Department of Education regarding certification. All applicants must qualify for state certification prior to employment.

The district does not discriminate on the basis of age, race, color, religion, sex, marital status, handicap, or natural origin.

BOTH MALES AND FEMALES ARE URGED TO APPLY

An Equal Opportunity Employer

FOR OFFICE USE ONLY
PHOTO (Required upon Employment)

PERSONAL DATA *(Please type or print)*

1. Name _____ 2. Social Security No. _____

3. Other names used _____ Dates of usage _____

4. Home mailing address: 5. Business mailing address:

   Street _____   Street _____

   City _____ State _____   City _____ State _____

   Zip _____ Phone _____   Zip _____ Phone _____

   Message Phone(s) _____

6. POSITION DESIRED:

   ELEMENTARY: (Grades K-6) List in order of preference.

   1. _____ 2. _____ 3. _____ 4. _____

   SECONDARY: List subject area preferences and total semester hours acquired in each area.

   Junior High (Grades 7-9)

   1. _____ _____   2. _____ _____   3. _____ _____
           Hours   Hours   Hours
   Senior High (Grades 10-12)

   1. _____ _____   2. _____ _____   3. _____ _____
           Hours   Hours   Hours

7. When will you be available? _____

8. Present Position _____ Salary _____

9. Reason for leaving present position _____

   _____

10. Present (or most recent) administrative supervisor(s):

   _____

11. Have you ever been dismissed from a position? *(Please circle)*   Yes   No

   If yes, explain _____

   _____

12. Have you ever been asked to resign from a position? *(Please circle)*   Yes   No

   If yes, explain _____

   _____

CERTIFICATION

13. State certificates now held:

CERTIFICATES	EXPIRATION DATE

14. State certificates for which you are eligible: *(Candidates are responsible for obtaining proper certification.)*

_____

_____

15. Location of university placement records and file: *(Give complete addresss)*

_____

_____

EDUCATIONAL PREPARATION ("See resume" is not sufficient)

16. School(s) attended:

NAME OF SCHOOL	LOCATION	NUMBER OF YEARS ATTENDED	DATES	GRADUATION YEAR	DEGREE
ELEMENTARY					
HIGH SCHOOL					
UNDERGRADUATE					
GRADUATE					
GRADUATE					

Highest degree earned: _____ Graduate semester hours earned **after** highest degree: _____

Undergraduate major: _____ _____ Undergraduate minor: _____ _____
                                          GPA   GPA

Graduate degree(s) in: _____ _____ _____ _____
                                              GPA   GPA

College activities in which you participated: _____

_____

_____

_____

PROFESSIONAL EXPERIENCE

17. STUDENT TEACHING EXPERIENCE

NAME OF SCHOOL	LOCATION		GRADES OR SUBJECT TAUGHT	DATES	COOPERATING TEACHER
	CITY	STATE			

18. CONTRACTUAL TEACHING ONLY: List most recent experience first and indicate whether position was full-time (FT) or part time (PT) equivalency. DO NOT *list substitute teaching experience.* ("See resume" is not sufficient.)

NAME & TYPE OF SCHOOL (Elem./Jr. High/Sr. High/etc.)	COMPLETE ADDRESS (street, city, state, zip)	GRADE(S) or SUBJECT(S) TAUGHT	NO. YRS.		DATES		REASON FOR LEAVING
			FT	PT	Beginning	Ending	

(List additional years on separate sheet)

19. OTHER WORK EXPERIENCE: List most recent experience first.

EMPLOYER	LOCATION	NATURE OF WORK	DATES

ACTIVITIES AND HONORS

20. Describe your special abilities or talents (e.g., sports, drama, etc.) _____

_____

_____

21. List professional organizations to which you belong _____

_____

_____

22. List leadership positions which you have held in various organizations _____

_____

_____

23. List honors received _____

_____

_____

16

REFERENCES:

24. Give names and complete addresses of three references who are familiar with your personality, character and work performance.

NAME	YEARS KNOWN	OFFICIAL POSITION	ADDRESS			
			STREET	CITY	STATE	PHONE

PROFESSIONAL GROWTH:
Please fill out in your own **handwriting**. If more room is needed, attach separate sheet.

25. Briefly state:
    (a) your reasons for desiring to teach in "ALL TOWN".
    (b) your plans for professional growth.
    (c) your educational goals for the future.
    (d) your philosophy of education.
    (e) your special qualifications for the position.
    (f) any additional information which you have not been able to include elsewhere on the application.

CONVICTION REPORT:

26. Because of the tremendous responsibility All Town School District has to its students and community, the following information is needed from all applicants and employees regarding convictions.* A record on conviction does not prohibit employment; however, failure to complete this form accurately and completely may mean disqualification from consideration for employment or may be cause for consideration of dismissal if employed and may result in prosecution for filing false information with a public agency. Applicants and employees must report any convictions that occur subsequent to the time they initally completed this form. Questions regarding this information should be directed to the Assistant Superintendent of Personnel. Please read carefully, and answer every question. **Please print clearly.**

a. Name (last, first, middle) _____

    Other names used _____ Dates of usage _____

b. Social Security Number _____

c. Have you ever been convicted of a minor offense other than traffic violation(s)?   YES   NO

d. Have you ever been convicted of a felony?   YES   NO

e. Have you ever been convicted of a sex or drug related offense?   YES   NO

f. Have you ever been convicted of a dangerous crime against children as defined in A.R.S. 13.604.01?**   YES   NO

If any of the boxes above are marked "YES," fill in the information below and attach a letter of explanation.

CONVICTION INFORMATION

1. CONVICTION CHARGE		DATE OF CONVICTION	COURT OF CONVICTION
CITY	STATE	AMOUNT OF FINE	LENGTH OF JAIL TERM
REMARKS:		LENGTH AND TERMS OF PROBATION:	

2. CONVICTION CHARGE		DATE OF CONVICTION	COURT OF CONVICTION
CITY	STATE	AMOUNT OF FINE	LENGTH OF JAIL TERM
REMARKS:		LENGTH AND TERMS OF PROBATION:	

* **CONVICTION** means the final judgment on a verdict or a finding of guilty, or a plea of *nolo contendere*, in any state or federal court of competent jurisdiction in a criminal case, regardless of whether an appeal is pending or could be taken. Conviction does **not** include a final judgment which has been expunged by pardon, reversed, set aside, or otherwise rendered invalid.

** A.R.S. 13.604.01 requires applicants to give notice of any conviction for dangerous crimes against children. These crimes are defined as second degree murder, aggravated assault, molestation of a child, sexual conduct with a minor, commercial sexual exploitation of a minor, sexual exploitation of a minor, child abuse, kidnapping and sexual abuse.

Under penalty of prosecution and dismissal, I hereby certify that the information presented on this application is true, accurate and complete. I authorize the investigation of all statements contained herein and understand that any document relevant to this information may be reviewed by the agents of All Town School District. I authorize the All Town School District to make reference checks prior to employment and I will execute such documents to facilitate this investigation. **I understand that my employment is not finalized until the background investigation has been completed and the Governing Board has officially approved my employment. I understand that misrepresentation or omission of pertinent facts may be cause for dismissal.**

_____   _____
SIGNATURE   DATE

Example B

ANYTOWN SCHOOL DISTRICT
Application Form (Certificated Personnel)
TEACHER APPLICATION SUPPLEMENT

A form similar to this might be included with the official Job Application Form. The purpose of this form is to reveal candidates' written communication skills as well as their attitudes about teaching.

1. Why do you want to be a teacher?

_____

_____

_____

_____

_____

_____

2. What do you want to accomplish as a teacher?

_____

_____

_____

_____

_____

_____

_____

3. How will (do) you go about finding out about students' attitudes and feelings about your class?

_____

_____

_____

_____

_____

_____

_____

4. An experienced teacher offers you the following advice: "Don't smile until Christmas."
   How do you feel about this?

_____

_____

_____

_____

_____

_____

5 What issues or concerns do you consider when you develop your lessons?

_____

_____

_____

_____

_____

_____

6. A parent comes to you and complains that the way you are teaching his child is inappropriate.
   How would you respond?

_____

_____

_____

_____

_____

_____

Step 4: District-Level Initial Screening Interview

Initial Screening Interview — When your file emerges from the paper screening, you will then be asked to appear in person for a formal, structured screening interview. This interview is often conducted by the personnel staff or district administrators.

The purpose of the structured interview is to ask the same questions of each candidate so that valid comparisons of the quality of responses can be determined. The structured screening interview allows the district personnel to determine what the applicant thinks and how well he/she can communicate ideas. Furthermore, the district personnel have defined attitudes, behaviors, and model responses that are anticipated by successful candidates. The structured screening allows the district to make these decisions. The questions generally take three forms: situational, observational, and personal.

Situational Questions—the applicant will be asked to respond to a specific classroom situation.

Example:

A group of students asks if it may organize a week-long course of study. This would require a change in your plans. What would you do?

Observational Questions—the applicant will be asked to reflect upon the action of a third party.

Example:

Some students have been disruptive in a third grade class. They are reassigned to another third grade teacher and she refuses to take them. What are your thoughts regarding the decision of the teacher?

Conceptual Questions—the applicant will be asked about beliefs, personal philosophy, and intentions as a teacher.

Example:

How do you generate excitement about what you are teaching? or, How would you assist in the development of a student's self-esteem?

Interviews: Predictors of Teacher Success

Perhaps the most important instructional decision a school district will make is hiring competent teachers. In fact, Boyles and Engel (1986) warn administrators, "The most important impact you can have on school quality is your hiring of teachers. The better your teachers, the better your schools." Thus, districts commit a great deal of time, energy, and resources to ensure only the best applicants are considered for positions in their schools.

Districts, seeking ways to predict who will be successful teachers, have worked to determine reliable and valid indicators of effective teachers. The indicators had to be measurable and identifiable through the course of a teacher interview. Though behavioral traits/characteristics of effective teachers are highly complex, Project EMPATHY (Thayer, 1978) revealed eight life themes (indicators) that can be discerned through the interview process. These themes are:

Relationship

A teacher with a strong relationship theme possesses good relating skills, such as listening, patience, and caring, and sees the building of relationships as the best way to help students grow and develop.

Democratic Orientation

A teacher with a democratic orientation works out problems with the students and sees supervision as supportive and understanding. This person does not deal with problems in an authoritarian manner.

Rapport Drive

This theme can be conceptualized as a teacher's ability to develop an approving and favorable relationship with each student. This teacher likes students and wants them to like him/her. Teachers with high rapport drive make you feel comfortable when you are around them.

Empathy

Empathy is the apprehension of the state of mind of another person. Practically, we say we put ourselves into the other person's place. We "feel" with him/her. Empathy is the phenomenon that provides the teacher feedback about the individual student's feelings and thoughts.

Student Orientation

This theme is basically a belief that students ought to be heard, understood, and dealt with as people first; and curriculum, materials, public image, etc. ought to take second place.

Acceptance

Acceptance is the ability to take a person "as is" and thus be prepared to help the person from that point. It is neither a condemn nor condone approach. It has been defined as "unconditional regard." Accepting teachers very often have an "openness" about their feelings that makes them more approachable.

Student Success

A teacher with this theme receives satisfaction from the success of students and sees student success as fulfillment of his/her goals.

Work and Profession Orientation

This theme includes a variety of areas: work organization, professional relationships, and belief in his/her profession.

During the structured screening interview, the objective of the interviewer is to get to know the applicant as thoroughly as possible. The interviewer will listen in an open, accepting manner, but will not generally probe or interject personal bias. Listening becomes the major behavior of the effective interviewer.

Hints to the Applicant

Know yourself as a teacher. Have a well thought out, consistent, basic, conceptual view of yourself as a teacher.

Be yourself. If you are trying to play a role which is not actually you, the interviewer will pick up the clues immediately. Remember, most interviewers have interviewed hundreds of candidates before you and have a broad experience base for comparison. By being your authentic self, the interview can be a pleasure for you, and the interviewer will be able to understand you more fully in a positive, open atmosphere.

Ask questions. Don't be afraid to ask that questions be repeated. Although the interviewer will not interpret questions for you (it is your interpretations which are important), the interviewer does want you to understand the questions.

Be spontaneous. Generally, the interviewers are not asking for a lot of detailed explanation of your basic position. Say what you think in as clear a manner as possible. Do not be afraid to change your point of view if you gain new insights during your process of thinking.

Be relaxed. Yes, the interview is structured, but this only means there are specific questions to be asked. You can unstructure the interview as much as you like by adding new insights or going back to previous questions at any time during the interview session.

Step 5: Principal's Selection Interview

Generally, the final step in the hiring process is the principal's selection interview. The purpose of this interview is to determine which of the candidates that are qualified for the job will be the "best fit" for the principal's school. Through the selection interview the principal attempts to learn about the candidate's beliefs and instructional practices. To find the best fit, the principal will need to be able to answer the following questions about the candidate at the end of the interview.

- Does the candidate possess the instructional skills we need?
- Will the candidate be a good classroom manager?
- Does the candidate share my vision of the school?
- Would the candidate be an asset to the school?
- Does the candidate possess enthusiasm, initiative, and sensitivity?
- Does the candidate project a love of teaching and learning?

To answer these questions, the principal will ask the candidate a number of probing, open-ended questions, take notes on the content/quality of the candidate's responses, and observe the candidate's communication skills and nonverbal mannerisms.

Your responsibility, as the candidate, is to present yourself in a professional manner, answer interview questions completely, and use your teaching portfolio to provide concrete examples of lesson plans, units and instructional activities. (For more information, see Section B: First Impressions: The Power of Presence, in this chapter).

Following are examples of the types of questions that a principal might ask during a selection interview. These questions are designed to elicit thoughtful, problem-solving responses that reveal the candidate's experiences and educational philosophy (Bratton 1990; O'Hair 1989; Armstrong 1988).

Interview Questions

- How do you help students develop a positive attitude about school?

- What behaviors might lead you to think a student may have a learning problem?

- What special attributes would you bring to this position?

- What are your priorities in teaching?

- What are some of the most innovative things you have attempted with students?

- Describe a responsibility you had at a prior teaching position and tell how you organized and managed it.

- What journals have given you useful professional information?

- If you could pick one goal for your students, what would it be?

- If you could pick one goal for yourself, what would it be?

- How would you challenge the gifted students in your room?

- How would you handle a student who continually disrupts your class?

- How would you try to motivate reluctant learners?

- What do you like most about teaching?

- Describe an event at school that frustrated you. How did you handle it?

- Tell me what your thoughts are on peer coaching.

- Under what conditions would you contact a parent?

- How would you get a restless student back on task?

Preparing for the Selection Interview

LEARN the principal's name and use it.
Be aware of titles, i.e. . . . Dr., Mr., Mrs.

ARRIVE EARLY, and double check the location for the interview. Have change for phone calls and parking.

KNOW something about the school, i.e. size, grade levels, approximate ethnic composition. Find out about the communities it serves by contacting city offices.

ASK questions. A serious candidate is curious about the position and is interested in the details of the job/school.

During the course of the selection interview, you will be expected to ask questions regarding the specific position for which you are interviewing. The following are examples of the type of questions you might wish to ask the principal.

Possible Candidate's Questions

What type of resources does the district/school provide for gifted, special needs, and bilingual/second language students?

What type of staff development program does the district have for beginning teachers?

Tell me about the instructional strengths of this school.

What are some of the challenges this school faces?

What type of discipline approach does this school use?

What resources are available to _____(content/grade) teachers?

Developing and Using A Teacher Portfolio

One dynamic method to document your strengths as a teacher is to develop a teaching portfolio. Since portfolios include multiple sources/types of data, they provide a rich portrayal of teacher development. A portfolio is a living document that records a teacher's evolution and provides an opportunity for reflection on developing practice. When used in an interview, portfolios allow a teacher candidate to demonstrate unique teaching style and philosophy in authentic context.

Portfolios should include actual artifacts of teaching/learning and written paragraphs reflecting on the meaning of these class-room activities and products. Teachers may include evaluations, video tape of teaching/learning activities, lesson/unit development, snapshots of classroom life, and products the students have developed. The display of the materials depends upon the unique tastes of its creator. Portfolios may be contained in a scrapbook or in a "treasure chest," depending on your interests and grade level.

Reflection paragraphs should include:

- Label of product/activity

- Use of product/activity

- Brief description of how product was developed or what purpose the activity served

- What the teacher/students learned from the product/activity

- How and why the teacher would modify the product or activity in the future

Section B

First Impressions: The Power of Presence

"Within the first two minutes of any personal meeting with somebody who has the power to hire you or screen you out of the hiring process, the decision has pretty much been made. That's how strongly first impressions affect the hiring decision." (Robert Half, founder of Robert Half and Accountemps).

When school districts hire teachers, they employ people who immediately inspire the public's trust and confidence. Therefore, among the critical factors district personnel consider when they interview potential teachers are those first visual impressions the candidate makes. Career Track researchers state that interviewers make lasting judgments based on first impressions, and first impressions are made in moments... only 3–7 seconds! Therefore, the clothing the candidate wears and the nonverbal behavior he/she exhibits are critical to success or failure in the interview process.

Jeers!

Cheers!

The Power of Presence

"If your clothing doesn't convey the message that you are competent, able, ambitious, self-confident, reliable and authoritative, nothing you say or do will overcome the negative signals emanating from your apparel." (Betty Harragan, "Games Mother Never Taught You"). John T. Molloy, author of "Dress for Success," agrees, and strongly recommends to people who are interviewing for professional positions, that their attire and demeanor must be conservative and business-like.

A great deal of research has been conducted by the business community to determine what colors, clothes, and styles, in particular, make the best first impression. The following are some suggestions for both men and women.

- Wear a classic suit; dark colors are best (dark blue or gray)

- Contrasting blouse/shirt (white, light blue)

- Men — a traditional red or dark blue tie

- Women — a red or dark blue scarf, or pocket handkerchief

- Men — matched-to-suit socks and shoes

- Women — Neutral stockings and matched-to-suit classic pump shoes

- Jewelry (watches, necklaces), simple, conservative, classic

- Carry materials in brief case or attache, not a book bag

- Scents — very light or none at all

- Hair — clean, and styled to show as much of the face/eyes as possible

> **Appearance is the #1 reason why teacher candidates aren't hired.**

Demeanor and Mannerisms:
The Power of Communication

Certain behaviors and mannerisms signal self-confidence and competence to potential employers. By the same token, other actions are perceived by interviewers as indicators of professional/personal inadequacy. The following are descriptions of behaviors on opposite ends of the continuum. During an interview, which would best describe you?

Competent Actions	Inadequate Actions
Voice	
Clear, firm tone of voice	Soft, hesitant, whispery voice
Positive, confirming statements	Questioning tone at end of responses
Variation in tone and pitch	Monotone, minimal inflection
Clear articulation	Mumbling, hesitation
Body	
Direct eye contact	Shifting eyes or glaring
Firm handshake	Limp, weak handshake
Appropriate, relaxed gestures	Fidgeting, nervous movement
Well balanced, straight posture	Stooped posture
Open, positive facial expressions	Frowning or smiling too much
Assured manner	Lip biting/furrowed brows
Enthusiastic, high energy level	Lethargic, low energy level

> **To project the most confident image, it may be necessary to practice interviewing with peers and family.**

References

Armstrong, C. (1988). Interview advice: Grill teachers about their track records. *The Executive Educator.* September, 29.

Bratton, R. (1990). How to conduct a successful job interview. *Principal* 69 (4), 50-51.

Boyles, N.L. & Engel, R.A. (1986). Finding teachers is tough: Hiring the right ones is tougher. *The Executive Educator.* August, 22-23.

Harragan, B.L. (1977). Games mother never taught you. New York: Warner Books, Inc.

Molloy, J.T. (1988). Dress for success. New York: Warner Books, Inc.

O'Hair, M. (1989). Teacher employment interview: A neglected reading. *Action in Teacher Education.* 11(1), 53-57.

Thayer, V.W. (1978). Project EMPATHY: An alternative way to hire teachers. North Central Association Quarterly. 52(Spring), 438-442.

Chapter 2

Putting It Together for the First Time

Section A:

Management of Time and Tasks

Determining, Teaching, and Reinforcing Routine Tasks

Teaching Routines

Task Analysis

Lightening the Load: Student Helpers

Section B:

The Paper Avalanche

Section C:

Preparing for School: Mental Check Lists

Section D:

Designing a Lesson Plan Book

The Long Haul to the Here and Now:
 Realities of Lesson Planning

Weekly/Daily Lesson Planning

Thematic Units

Lesson Plan Evaluation: Time for Reflection

References

Putting It Together

Have you ever put together a thousand piece jigsaw puzzle without a sample of the completed picture? That is how a beginning teacher described her efforts to organize and manage her classroom.

What you do during the first few days of the school year may predict both teacher and student success. As a pre-service teacher, you may not have had the opportunity to observe a veteran teacher establish his/her classroom at the start of the school year. Therefore, this chapter is devoted to reviewing basic management routines, organizing materials and resources, and lesson planning.

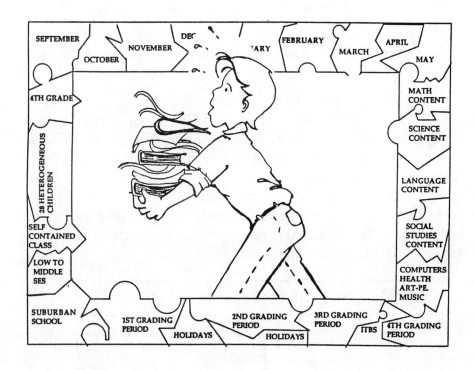

Section A

Management of Time and Tasks

All classrooms have routines that must be performed on a daily basis. Successful veteran teachers recommend that beginning teachers should:

- ☞ Identify the routine tasks that will be needed in their classroom.

- ☞ Decide exactly how each task will be accomplished (analysis).

- ☞ Determine how and when they will teach these tasks directly.

Experienced teachers and classroom effectiveness researchers (Emmer & Evertson, 1980; Sanford and Evertson, 1980) suggest that the establishment of these routines should begin on the first day of school and continue through the first week or two of school. In other words, routine tasks are taught first, rather than academic content. Experienced teachers stress that taking advantage of this time to teach routines will actually give you more total teaching time during the year, plus the benefit of having a well-managed, organized classroom.

1st Week Plan	9-10	10-11	11-12	12-1	1-2	2-3
Monday	Signals		Lunch Routines		End of Day	
Tuesday	Entering Routines		Rules of Respect		Supplies Routine	
Wednesday	Attendance		Music		Stoplight Talking	
Thursday			PE			
Friday			Art			

Determining, Teaching, and Reinforcing
Routine Tasks

A teacher might select dozens of possible routines to help make classroom life easier and more organized. The trick is knowing which ones are the most useful for you and your class. Cummings (1983) suggests that teachers begin the very first few seconds of the first day by teaching a "pay attention signal." This "get their attention" signal should be auditory, simple, but effective. Here are a few examples of auditory signals:

Primary Grades

- counting to five
- clapping hands in a rhythm
- ringing a bell

Intermediate/Secondary Level

- saying special signal words, such as, "Listen," "Ready," "Class."
- saying special signal phrases, such as, "I need your attention."

Another category of signals you can use with all age levels are the silent, nonverbal, visual signals. These silent signals "speak volumes" and clearly communicate your message in an instant, if you teach their meaning. Here are some examples of nonverbal, silent, and visual signals that may be used for a variety of purposes:

- five finger countdown
- an "OK" sign
- index finger to your lips for silence
- facial expressions/eye contact/body language
- switch light off and on

Like verbal/auditory signals, the meaning of each of these signals must be explicitly taught, practiced, and reinforced until they become routine habits.

Teaching Routines

Teaching the signal (or any routine procedure) means that you tell the students directly what the signal will be, what it will be used for, and what they must do when they hear it. For example:

Rationale and Set: "Class, there are many times in a day when I will need to have your attention very quickly."

Specific Information and Modeling: "When I need you to be quiet and listen, I will count to five. By the time I count to five, you should have put down whatever it is you are doing, stop talking, look at me, and listen to the directions I give next."

Guided Practice: "Let's practice this right now. 1, 2, 3 — everyone should stop talking and put down anything you are doing, put down your pencil if you are writing, put down your book if you are reading — 4 and 5, look at me."

Independent Practice: "Throughout the day I will be using our 'pay attention signal,' and I'll be checking to see who knows what to do."

Auditory Signals

Pay Attention Signal — "5 - Fingers" Visual Signal

Task Analysis

After you have identified which routine tasks you need to teach and when you are going to teach them, you then will need to consider how you plan to teach these routines. Each behavior or routine should be task-analyzed before being taught. Specifically, the skill of task analysis involves:

1. Identifying "content" — what do students need to know and what do they need to be able to do.

2. Sequencing — what skills/actions need to logically occur first, second, third, etc.

The following are examples of content and sequencing of routine tasks.

Pencil Exchange Routine

Students may not sharpen their pencils during instruction. Sharpened pencils are kept in a pencil exchange container (points up). Students may exchange dull or broken pencils before class begins.

(Pencils are sharpened during breaks by the student assigned to this task.)

Leaving the Room

Students who need to use the bathroom or go to the office or special class during class time must:

Take the appropriate pass. (bathroom, office/nurse, errand)

Place their name clip or magnet on the picture or label that identifies their destination.

Replace their name clip or magnet when re-entering the classroom.

Study Buddy

- ✏ Each student identifies one person to be a study buddy.

- ✏ The buddies exchange phone numbers.

- ✏ When a student is absent, the buddy completes a "While You Were Gone" form.

- ✏ That night the absent buddy calls the "study buddy" and receives the assignments/information that were missed.

(Teacher may wish to facilitate this by encouraging students who live near each other to become buddies. Teacher keeps the buddy list posted. Assignments and reminders are given by the student assigned to coordinate study buddies.

Absent Student Assignment Form

Name _____ Date(s) _____ _____

While

    You

        Were

            Gone

Subject	Assignment(s)	When Due

Deciding what routines to teach, how to teach them, and when to teach them is critical. The charts that follow are examples of routines that can be taught during the first week of school.

Primary Pointers

Monday: pay attention signal

bathroom procedures

lunch ticket routine

lining up

Tuesday: entering classroom procedures

attendance

getting materials

returning completed work (mail box)

Wednesday: pencil sharpening/pencil exchange can

drinking fountain/batters box

"stoplight" talking rule

rules of respect

working independently

Thursday: finishing work early

seeking teacher help

fire drill

to and from playground

Friday: classroom helpers

appropriate learning center behavior

end of day and daily clean up activities

study buddy system (missing class)

Intermediate Interests and Secondary Specialities

Just because students are older, do not assume that they will automatically know what you want or expect. Like primary teachers, intermediate and secondary teachers must also explicitly teach the routine tasks and procedures they wish to use in their classrooms.

Monday: Baseline Behaviors and Expectations

- attention signal
- rules of respect
- entering and exiting classroom routines

Tuesday: Policies and Procedures during Instruction

- student behavior during instruction
- seeking teacher's attention/help
- student behavior during independent seat-work
- using classroom supplies (pencils, texts)

Wednesday: Assignment Expectations/Homework

- quality of work
- turning in work

Thursday: Assignment Expectations (continued)

- assignment calendar
- make-up/absence procedures (Study Buddy)
- checking/grading policies

Friday: Special Concerns

- activities to do when work has been completed
- classroom cleanup
- fire drill

Lightening the Load: Student Helpers

As you can see by the examples on the previous pages, implementation and management of routine activities are taught by you, but maintained by the students in your room. After you have identified, taught and established routine tasks, your next step is to decide what tasks you can delegate to the students in your room.

Student helpers can make classroom life easier for you and more fun and important for them. Even middle and secondary students enjoy helping. The following is a list of possible student tasks. Some jobs are more primary, while others are appropriate for older students.

Class Secretary	Assignment Calendar
Paper Passer	Study Buddy Monitor
Packet Makers	Lunch Chart Monitor
Classroom Librarian	Line Leader
Pencil Sharpener	Errand Runner

Veteran's View: *After you have taught the first helpers the tasks, they can be responsible for teaching the next person the details of that specific duty. This saves you even more time.*

Whatever jobs you decide upon, be sure that all students have an opportunity to perform the tasks. As before, you will need to teach specifically what the job entails. After you have done this, you can save hours of time and have a well-managed and organized classroom that benefits both you and your students.

Section B

The Paper Avalanche

Organizing your classroom and managing the paper avalanche that awaits all teachers is a real challenge for beginning teachers. This section provides suggestions that will help you manage your time and materials.

Managing Time — Schedule your time into two separate areas: School and Home. When teachers get into the habit of taking school work home, they often begin to feel "overwhelmed" with teaching. No wonder teachers often feel that teaching is a twenty-four hour a day job! In addition, it is also important to learn how to make the most of your time at school. You will be amazed at how much you can accomplish in even the briefest preparation times and breaks if you are an efficient time manager.

Calendar — Purchase a large calendar (the "month at a glance" type). Record school and personal activities immediately and up-date daily. Carry your calendar with you. Get in the habit of blocking out scheduled personal and family time.

Mail — Read through mail/memos at the end of the day. Throw away junk mail. Record important dates and deadlines on your calendar immediately, then throw the actual notice away (or place in your recycle box). File important documents and respond to any requests as soon as possible, instantaneously if possible. Consider this guiding principle: Handle any piece of paper only ONE TIME!

After school — Establish an efficient after school routine. Save time by knowing what needs to be done and then do it.

Assigning Homework — Develop an assignment calendar chalkboard or bulletin board. Again use a student helper to keep the assignment calendar current.

> *Mentor's Memo:*
> *Make an individual as-signment calendar for students to keep in notebooks.*
> *Either weekly (primary grades) or monthly (middle and high school). This encourages organizational and time-managment skills and helps students become more responsible for their assignments.*

The next two pages provide models of how you might wish to organize assignment calendars.

Assignment Calendar

Assignments for the Week of _____

Name of Student _____

	Monday	Tuesday	Wednesday	Thursday	Friday
English					
Math					
Reading					
Science					
Social Studies					
Spelling					
Library/ Computer Lab					
Art					
Music					
PE					
Notes					

Monthly Assignment Calendar

Student Name _____ Class _____ Month _____

Mon.	Tues.	Wed.	Thurs.	Fri.	Sat.	Sun

*Student write in the appropriate dates.

Collecting homework or permission slips, field trip money, etc. can become very time consuming, unless you are prepared for the task. Using a generic check-in form is an easy way to manage this chore—and, it, too, can be assigned to a student helper.

1.   Simply make multiple check-in forms with the student names (alphabetically ordered) already written in the blanks.

2.   When the students return their homework, permission slips, etc., simply check off their names.

3.   The "check-in" form is then clipped to the materials that have been returned.

4.   Use the column for notes/comments if you need to "re-send" any information or if student is delayed for a particular reason.

Names	Permission Slips
Ravi	x
Geri	
Alice	x
Pam	x
Mary Jo	x
Karen	
Sharad	
Kristine	x
John	
Billie	

Generic Check-In Form

Activity _____ Date _____

Student Name(s)   Notes/Comments

_____

_____

_____

_____

_____

_____

_____

_____

_____

_____

_____

_____

_____

_____

_____

_____

_____

_____

_____

_____

Section C

_____
_____
_____

Preparing for the opening of school can be one of the most stressful times for all teachers. Beginning teachers, particularly, find that the opening days and weeks of school are emotionally and physically taxing.

Developing and using check lists to help organize your thoughts may also help organize your efforts and maximize your time.

The following section provides a number of "mental check lists" which may assist your planning.

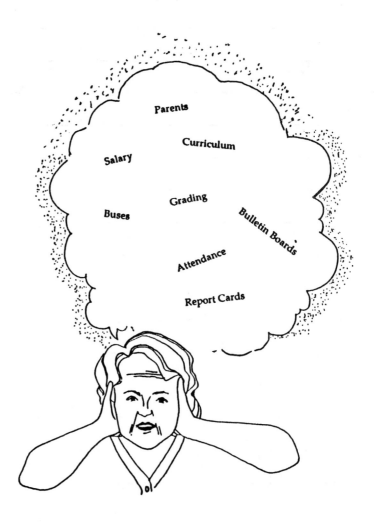

Preparing for School — Mental Check List:

Classroom and Lesson Preparation	Notes

If you have your own classroom:

_____ Make bulletin boards:

     _____monthly calendar

     _____assignment calendar

     _____announcements

     _____student work display

     _____welcome back

     _____subject interest displays

post: fire drill list, bus roster, emergency #s

_____ Plan to have students assist
     with bulletin boads.

_____ Organize your desk and filing system

_____ Prepare first week's lesson plan

_____ Begin to establish substitute folder

If you are a "traveling" teacher:

_____ If possible, locate a place in each room where
     you can store large supplies and materials.

_____ Organize a brief case or small suitcase
     for use as a traveling teaching kit.

Preparing for School — Mental Check List:

Student Preparation	Notes

_____ Prepare class rosters and
     permanent record folders

_____ Make age-appropriate name tags.

_____ Prepare parent communique packets. Include:

    _____emergency forms

    _____school rules

    _____introduction letter

    _____needed supplies

    _____any district/school memos

_____ Prepare generic student check-in form

_____ Create "new student" packet that contains all
     initial information for students who transfer into
     your class throughout the year (make at least 12).

Preparing for School — Mental Check List:

Materials and Supplies	Notes

_____ Do you have all your texts?

    _____students' texts

    _____teachers' editions

    _____supplementary materials

_____ Are you familiar with your district's report card and the schedule for grading periods?

_____ Do you have all of your supplies and materials?

    _____plan book

    _____attendance materials

    _____grading book

    _____student folders

    _____pencils/crayons

    _____writing paper

    _____construction paper

    _____stapler/staples

    _____tape/glue

    _____scissors

    _____tacks and pins

    _____paper clips/rubber bands

Preparing for School — Mental Check List:

Routine and Procedures	Notes
_____ Have you decided on your class procedures and routines?	
_____ Have you considered when and how you are going to teach them?	
_____ What are the student jobs in your classroom?	
_____ Have you considered the rules of respect for your classroom?	
_____ Do you know what the school rules are, e.g. lunch room, playground?	
_____ Do you know when and how you are going to teach them?	
_____ Do you know where all special classes and facilities (library, nurse's office) are in your building?	
_____ Do you know what procedures are required to send students to these places?	

Section D

Designing A Lesson Plan Book

Your lesson plan book is one of the main keys to organizing and managing your time and the curriculum. Unfortunately, many beginning teachers find the standard commercial lesson plan book difficult to use, as it is often hard to put all of your thoughts in the small boxes typically provided. One suggestion that can be helpful is to develop an individualized lesson plan book that meets your specific needs.

In this section we have provided some models/samples of planning schemas and some suggestions that might help you organize critical information. Begin by purchasing a large (2" to 3") three-ring binder. Then copy any of the forms you believe to be useful, or modify or develop the forms that are more appropriate for your needs. Finally, organize the sections in your lesson plan book in a manner that makes the greatest sense for you. This type of planning book allows you the greatest flexibility and an opportunity to elaborate or adapt throughout your first year of teaching.

Possible Contents

- Class Roster(s)
- Seating Chart(s)
- Birthday Chart
- Calendar
- Long-Term Planning
- Daily Planning
- Student Grades
- Bus Roster

The Long Haul to the Here and Now: Realities of Lesson Planning

To begin "getting the whole picture," a new teacher should plan a tentative year-long overview. Knowing what lies ahead gives you an opportunity to **see** how you can make all the curricular pieces fit together, smoothly! To begin this process, we suggest that you first consult the district curriculum guide, and then discuss plans with a veteran teacher who teaches the same grade level or subject areas that you will be responsible for teaching.

Super Suggestion:
Be sure to include all vacation and district deadline/planning/in-service days (parent-teacher conferences, open house, 1/2 day schedules, etc.)

Mentor's Memo:
Consult this chart weekly as you create your weekly/daily lesson plans.

Long-term Planning Format

	Social Studies/Langauge Arts	**Science/Math**
September		
October		
November		
December		
January		
February		
March		
April		
May		

Example: Long-term Planning Kindergarten

	Social Studies/Langauge Arts	Science/Math
September	Open House 23 Me Unit Sidewalk Safety	Classification sizes/shapes/colors
October	Parent-Teacher Conference 23-26 Halloween Traditions Fire Safety	5 Senses/Hygiene Number Recognition
November	Veteran's Day 11 Family & Thanksiving Traditions	Dental Care Number Recognition
December	Christmas Vacation 18-3 Christmas Traditions	Poison Safety Patterning
January	Community Helpers	Winter Adaptations Addition 1 – 10
February	Valentine's & President's Day	Animal Unit Seriation 1 – 100
March	Animal Unit continues St. Patrick's Day Parent-Teacher Conference 13–16	Coin Recognition
April	Spring Break 10–15 Spring/Weather Watch/Season Study/ Hatching Chicks Plant Life Cycle and Butterfly Life Cycle/ Subtraction	
May	Summer/Water Safety	Ocean and Sea Life

Middle and secondary school teachers often have multiple class preparations. They may wish to use a long-range planning format when they are planning their year as well.

This type of long-range planning helps you maximize curricular integration, order resource/supplemental materials, and make the most effective use of instructional time. Planning like this also allows you an opportunity to space preparation and grading end-of-unit materials.

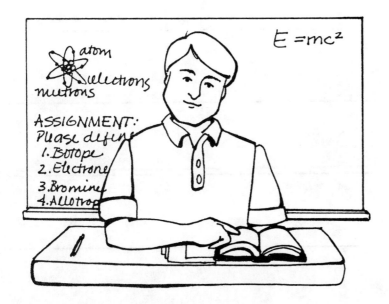

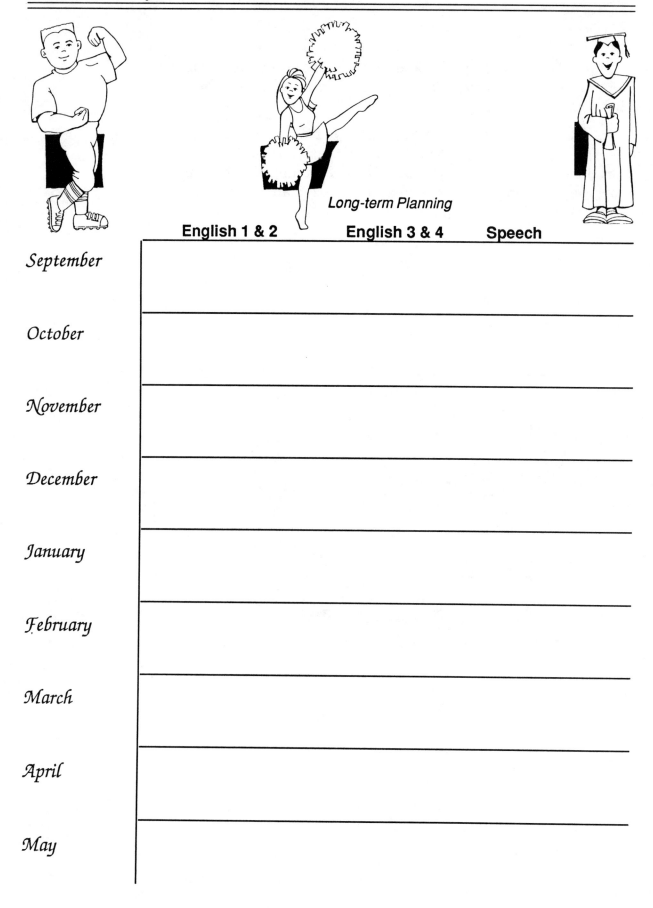

Long-term Planning

	English 1 & 2	English 3 & 4	Speech
September			
October			
November			
December			
January			
February			
March			
April			
May			

Weekly/Daily Lesson Planning

Sustained, Silent Planning Time — Since it is often more productive to develop your lesson plans in the classroom (all your material and resources are close at hand), plan to stay at school one day a week until your planning is completed. This practice also helps to reinforce a separate home and school life.

> **Super Suggestion:**
> Frequently, teachers' days are extremely tiring, both physically and mentally. Therefore, experienced teachers recommend that you arrange some planning time on the wekend, if necessary, rather than staying late at school each day.

Daily Lesson Plan

Week of	Notes	
Monday		
Tuesday		
Wednesday		
Thursday		
Friday		

Notes

Lesson Plan Development

Developing lesson plans means that you are basically developing answers to four questions:

1. What do you want the students to know or do?

2. What resources/materials will you use to teach this information?

3. What instructional techniques will you use to teach these concepts?

4. How will you determine the students' level of understanding?

Your lesson plan book usually serves as an outline/overview for the instructional events that will occur in your classroom. An actual "lesson plan" may often need to be more fully developed so that the beginning teacher has a blueprint for instruction.

Learner Outcomes: Instructional Objectives

Introduction: Focus and Anticipatory Set

Instructional Input: Teaching Procedures and Student Activities

Evaluation: Checking for Understanding and Lesson Assessment

Closure: Lesson Summation and Learner Participation

Resources: Equipment, Materials, Teaching Aids

Thematic Units

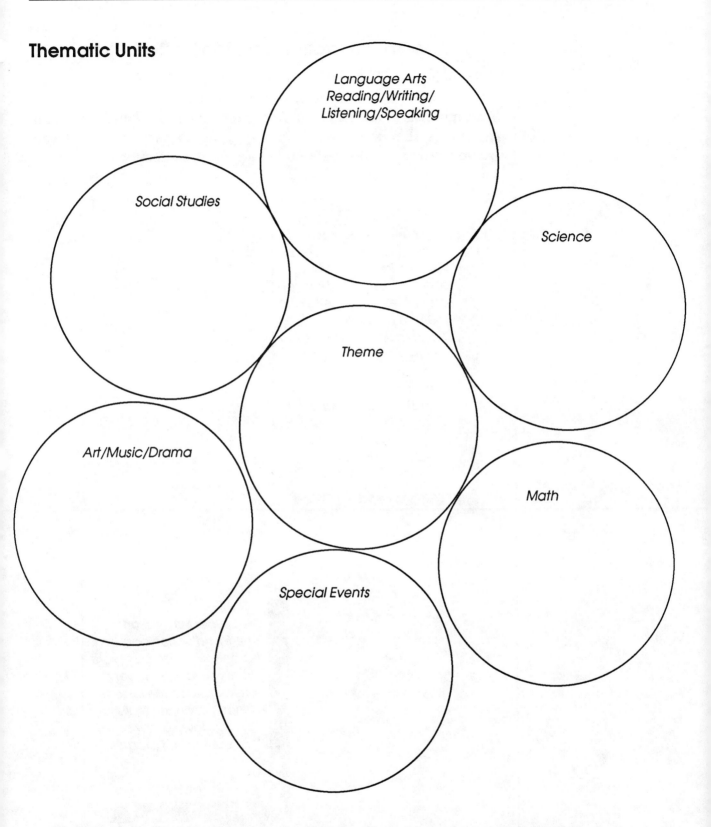

Another type of lesson planning may involve thematic units or integrated curricula. One way to represent this type of instructional strategy is to map subject areas.

Lesson Plan Evaluation: Time for Reflection

Time is one of a teacher's most valuable commodities. To continue to make the best use of your time, you will need to set aside 5–10 minutes at the end of each day for reflection. Think about all the things that went well and why; then think about what you would change about the day to make it more effective.

> **Mentor's Memos:**
> *It often helps to use your lesson plan itself to guide your reflection. Use a red ink pen to jot notes to yourself in the margins of the lesson plan. Did a lesson run significantly longer or shorter than you expected? Why? Did you get a "brainstorm" in the middle of instruction? Jot down the idea, to help you remember it again.*
> *Did you capitalize on a "teachable" moment?*

> **Super Suggestion:**
> *Time for reflection about the lesson will not be complete until you review students' responses to the lesson. Using your anecdotal stickers, jot down a few notes about student progress.*

Class Record

Student Name	Address	Telephone No.	Notes*
1.			
2.			
3.			
4.			
5.			
6.			
7.			
8.			
9.			
10.			
11.			
12.			
13.			
14.			
15.			
16.			
17.			
18.			
19.			
20.			
21.			
22.			
23.			
24.			
25.			
26.			
27.			
28.			
29.			
30.			

*Parents' last name, if different, guardianship rights

Student Grades

Subject:

Name	M	T	W	Th	F	M	T	W	Th	F	M	T	W	Th	F	M	T	W	Th	F
1.																				
2.																				
3.																				
4.																				
5.																				
6.																				
7.																				
8.																				
9.																				
10.																				
11.																				
12.																				
13.																				
14.																				
15.																				
16.																				
17.																				
18.																				
19.																				
20.																				
21.																				
22.																				
23.																				
24.																				
25.																				
26.																				
27.																				
28.																				
29.																				
30.																				

Bus List

Bus

Bus

Bus

Bus

Bus

Bus

Seating Chart

You may wish to lamintate this page and use a transparency marker to easily record where students are currently sitting.

References

Brooke, D.M., & Hawke, G. (1985). Effective and ineffective session opening: Teacher activity and task structures. Paper presented at the American Educational Research Association, Chicago.

Emmer, C., & Evertson, C. (1980). Effective management at the beginning of the school year in junior high classes. Research and Development Center for Teacher Education, The University of Texas, Austin.

Emmer, C., & Evertson, C. (1981). Synthesis of research on classroom management. *Educational Research*, 38(4), 341- 347.

Evertson, C.M., Emmer, E.T., Clements, B.S., Sanford, J.P., & Worsham, M.E. (1984). *Classroom Management for Elementary Teachers*. Englewood Cliffs, NJ. Prentice-Hall.

Kounin, J. (1970). Discipline and Groups Management in Classrooms. New York, Holt, Rinehart and Winston.

Sanford, J. & Evertson, C. (1980). Beginning the school year at a low SES junior high. Austin, Texas: Research and Development Center for Teacher Education.

Chapter 3

Public Relations
and the Beginning Teacher

Section A:

First Day Communiques

Open House

Section B:

Newsletter

News Flashes

Phone Calls

Section C:

Parent Teacher Conferences

Conference Scheduling

Portfolio Evaluation System

Observations and Anecdotal Notes

Parent Conference Format/Form

Avoiding Conference Confrontations

Managing Conference Confrontations

Setting the Scene

References

Section A

First Day Communique\Open House

Parents want to be informed! Whether you work with five or fifteen year old students, parents want to know about you, your classroom, and how their students are learning and behaving. Parents are your public, and your ability to relate to them is critical to your success. Good public relations means good communication and that doesn't just happen . . . it must be planned. There is no mystery to working with parents. They simply want to know:

- ✏ That you care about the academic, social and psychological welfare of their child.

- ✏ How their child is progressing and behaving in class.

- ✏ What they can realistically do to support their child's efforts.

The parents' perception of you as a caring professional and their knowledge of how to help their child cannot be developed in isolation. This chapter is devoted to helping you recognize and maximize communication opportunities.

First Day Communique

On the opening day of school, you have a wonderful opportunity to introduce yourself, establish class expectations and procedures, and ask for specific parental support. This First Day Communique should be upbeat and to the point. The tone should be friendly, and information should be stated positively.

Example:

"Students need to report to school between 8:00 and 8:30. School starts promptly at 8:30," not *"Don't send students before 8:00. Students are marked tardy after 8:30."*

Coach's Corner:
Like appearance, your first communique will make a lasting impression. Have a concerned colleague edit your work for grammar, spelling and most importantly a positive "tone."

Principal's Principles:
Have the principal read your section on behavior expectation/consequences to ensure that your classroom rules mirror (do not exceed or undermine) the behavior policies of the school.

Super Suggestion:
Students will enter your classroom throughout the year. To assist with their adjustment, make 12 - 15 extra First Day Communique and place in "New Student Files."

Veteran's Views:
To make sure the First Day Communique is read by parents, you should also include a detachable parent signature response/return form.

Primary Pointers

Start with an exciting cover that relates to your welcoming theme, such as "The A, B C's for a Happy Year."

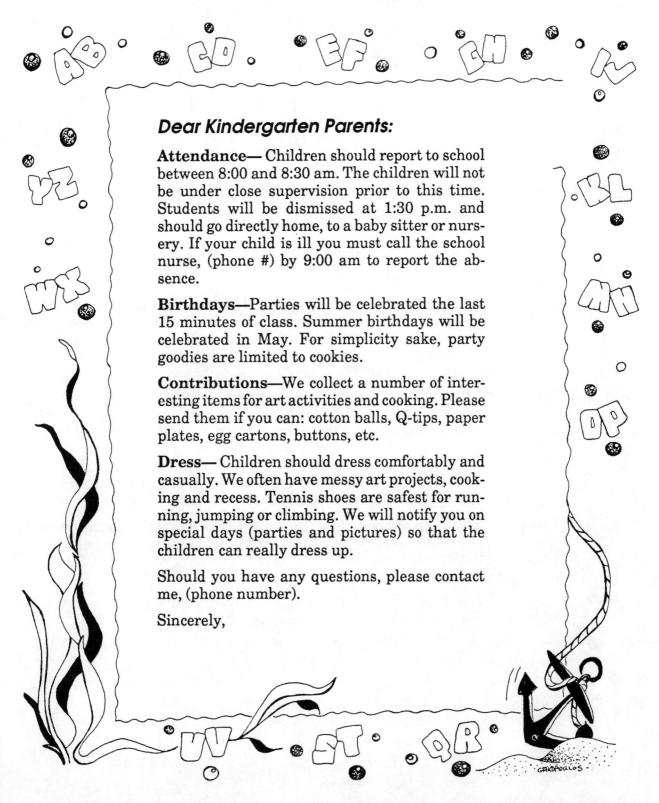

Dear Kindergarten Parents:

Attendance— Children should report to school between 8:00 and 8:30 am. The children will not be under close supervision prior to this time. Students will be dismissed at 1:30 p.m. and should go directly home, to a baby sitter or nursery. If your child is ill you must call the school nurse, (phone #) by 9:00 am to report the absence.

Birthdays—Parties will be celebrated the last 15 minutes of class. Summer birthdays will be celebrated in May. For simplicity sake, party goodies are limited to cookies.

Contributions—We collect a number of interesting items for art activities and cooking. Please send them if you can: cotton balls, Q-tips, paper plates, egg cartons, buttons, etc.

Dress— Children should dress comfortably and casually. We often have messy art projects, cooking and recess. Tennis shoes are safest for running, jumping or climbing. We will notify you on special days (parties and pictures) so that the children can really dress up.

Should you have any questions, please contact me, (phone number).

Sincerely,

Intermediate Interests and Secondary Specialities

Like primary teachers, intermediate and secondary teachers should also develop a First Day Communique that delineates specific classroom expectations, policies and procedures. Many experienced intermediate and secondary teachers suggest that reviewing this communique with students is a critical first day activity.

Dear Parents,

It is a pleasure to welcome your student to my History Class at Any Town High School.

Instructional format

My class will be a lecture class requiring notes to be taken every day. Once each week, discussion will be the required lesson of the day. I believe that students learn best about their future by reviewing and personalizing the past. Class participation, including oral reports, guest speakers (such as grandparents and parents), and oral thinking are encouraged.

Absences

Absences due to illness are to be made up after school the following day by outlining my lecture notes. After four absences, a conference is required with the parent, and after 10 days of absence the student will be dropped into a study hall with a loss of credit. If an extended absence occurs, it is imperative that you contact me immediately at (xxx-xxxx) after 3:00 p.m. and before 5:00 p.m. to make special arrangements.

Homework & grading

There will be 6 major tests and 9 quizzes each quarter in addition to the daily notes. I collect the notes on discussion day and return them the Monday after our "oral thinking" day. Grades are awarded on a curve from the daily notes, the tests, the quizzes, and the oral involvement. Each semester I require a major investigation into some point in history that we have reviewed, and ask that a 5 to 8 page report be prepared. I will also be sending homework reading two days each week.

I encourage discussion at home about the issue so that my goal of internalization can be assisted with your reflection. Students who do not turn in the paper will be given an incomplete grade until it is turned in.

Contacting teacher

If you need to call me, please do so during school hours and leave a message if I am in class. I will return your call as soon as possible.

Best wishes, and I look forward to meeting you personally at Open House, October 14, 1993 at 7:00 p.m. at Anytown High School.

Best wishes for a great year,

Bob Best
History Teacher

Open House

Meeting parents at the Open House can be exciting and intimidating. Most new teachers face this event nervously. However, the opportunity to meet parents personally is a great chance to strengthen your instructional efforts. To encourage attendance, it is important to formally invite parents early and remind them frequently of the day and time of the Open House.

Pointers for Primary Teachers

Veteran teachers have found you can almost guarantee parental attendance if you:

- ☛ Welcome the entire family (baby-sitters may be hard to find and expensive).

- ☛ Organize student presentations in your classroom (this requires coordination with other grade level/subject areas).

- ☛ Serve refreshments (ask for parent contributions).

- ☛ Hold drawings for door prizes (children's trade books, markers, fancy pencils, etc.).

Super School

Welcomes Your Family

to

Open House
Tuesday, September 12

Classroom Presentation Times
Kindergarten 7:00

First Grade 7:20

Second Grade 7:40

Third Grade 8:00

Join in our excitement for learning and sharing

Student entertainment
Door Prizes
Refreshments

See You There!!

Coach's Corner: Include map of school on the back of invitation.

Pointers for Primary Teachers

Guest Book—have parents sign in and fill out door prize drawing cards.

Class Quilt—children and teacher draw and label pictures of themselves. You arrange pictures in a quilt fashion. This creates a strong sense of classroom community.

Learning Centers—label each learning center and provide a handout that describes each center's educational importance. Post two or three students at each center to discuss and demonstrate center activities.

Parent Notes—all students write a welcome note to their family and place it on their desks or tables.

Teacher Presentation—Dress professionally and SMILE. Your presentation should be brief, positive and enthusiastic. Address issues such as daily schedules, classroom rules and expectations, learning centers, homework assignments, and special activities.

Provide a handout that summarizes the content of your presentation. This handout may need to be translated into other languages.

Students' Show—nothing fancy just a fun group effort! Children can present a choral poem, finger-play, song etc. No solos! This only increases the perceptions of bias or teacher's pet syndrome.

Intermediate Interests and Secondary Specifics

Open House at the intermediate and secondary level is a school-wide effort. Usually parents are sent a copy of each student's class schedule and are asked to attend a 15 – 20 minute orientation in each of their student's classes. There is generally a 5 – 7 minute passing period between each class. This organization allows the parents to "get a feel for" their student's day and an opportunity to meet each of the teachers. The school administration may host a general session at the beginning of the evening to introduce the administrative personnel and support staff and to present pertinent information about district and school policies regarding attendance and extra-curricular activities. At the intermediate and secondary levels, it is usually the responsibility of the administration to publicize the event, organize entertainment and provide refreshments.

Knowing how important it is to meet and talk with the parents, many intermediate and secondary teachers often use a number of activities to encourage the students to bring their parents to Open House.

- ☛ **Class Competitions** — Teachers hold a competition between all the classes they teach and the class with the most parents attending receives a pizza party, or a free period on Friday, or a "one time only" homework pass.

- ☛ **Door Prize** — Teacher encourages parents to complete an information card (see example next page) and drop it in a fish bowl. The teacher draws one or two cards per class and gives away items that carry the school's logo.

- **Teacher Presentation**—Dress professionally and SMILE. Your presentation should be concise, positive and enthusiastic. Veteran teachers recommend discussing grading and homework policies, class expectations, major units to be covered during the semester, and any special events that are forthcoming.

- **Handout**—Provide a handout that summarizes what you will be saying. This handout may need to be translated into other languages.

Example:

Student's Name _____ Age _____

Your name(s)   _____

Home # _____   Office # _____

Do you wish to make a private appointment? Yes ___ No ___

Best times for you to meet _____

Particular concerns _____

_____

_____

Principal's Principles: During your presentation, you need to offer an opportunity to parents to make an appointment with you if they wish to discuss student's progress individually. The form is a simple way of documenting their concerns and allows you to contact them later.

NOTES

Section B

Newsletters/Flashes/Phone Calls

"An ounce of prevention...." Communicating with parents can be done most effectively, with minimal time impositions, if done proactively. Establishing and maintaining a regular newsletter is essential. Your grade level and/or school policy will determine what "regular" means:

> Kindergarten through second grade — weekly
>
> Third through sixth grade — bimonthly
>
> Seventh through twelfth grade — monthly

Pointers for Primary Teachers

Primary Newsletters should:

- ✍ Be reader friendly, conversational, and not laden with educational jargon.

- ✍ Review, briefly, the high points of last week's learning.

- ✍ Preview the goals and activities planned for the coming week.

- ✍ Acknowledge a "thank you" to all parents or staff who supported your instructional efforts.

- ✍ Be sent home consistently on one particular day of the week. Mondays are generally best.

Example:

September 1,

Dear Kindergarten Parents

Last week was very busy! We continued the Sidewalk Safety unit. We reviewed the meaning of the "stop sign" and "traffic light" and have practiced "Stop, Look and Listen" before we crossed the streets with Mrs. Smith, our Crossing Guard, to be sure we get to school and home again safely.

This week we will begin our very important **ME** unit. To do this we will begin learning and/or practice writing our very special names. Mastering the art of printing requires much time, patience and practice. It takes lots of "exercise" to develop little finger muscles. At first, just the effort alone deserves encouragement and praise. MUCH LATER, as our little writers gain skill and confidence we can then begin to see really well formed words. But again, EN-COURAGEMENT of the effort is more important than the perfection of the printing.

We will need to have a set of play clothes that your child may wear when needed. This is for an EXTRA SPECIAL ME project. Please send the clothes in a large bag with your child's name on it by Friday. The clothes will be returned by Tuesday after Open House on September 20th, at 7:00 p.m.

A special THANK YOU goes to Mrs. Lane, Mrs. Angst, Mrs. Atkinson and Mrs. Corley for constructing Work Jobs learning activities for our classroom. The children are learning so much from working with these wonderful thinking tasks.

Thank you, also, for sharing your beautiful, eager and bright children with me.

Sincerely,

Interests of Intermediate Teachers

At this level, students can help to write the newsletters.

1. The last 15 – 20 minutes of the day, two or three times a week, students can review the day's learning and suggest their views of the most important and interesting events.

2. The teacher lists their responses on the board.

3. The students then individually choose a topic from the list, and each writes a short descriptive paragraph.

4. The teacher collects the paragraphs and assigns teams to peer edit.

5. The students peer edit each other's work. They have now become co-authors on two articles.

6. The teacher collects the edited works and uses them in the weekly or bimonthly newsletter.

This activity has several positive features:

- ✐ It serves as a closure-summarization activity each day.

- ✐ Students have an opportunity to practice writing brief, journalistic text.

- ✐ Students work together to edit and improve their own and others' writing skills.

- ✐ Each child in the classroom can co-author at least one article.

- ✐ Parents receive frequent communications about classroom activities from the student's perspective.

- ✐ Students have a regular and real chance to "publish" their works for others to read and appreciate.

Specifics for Secondary Teachers

Middle school and secondary teachers often assume that because their students are older and more verbal, students will share pertinent information about their classes with their parents. This is simply not the case. Most parents of middle and secondary students feel out of touch with the activities and requirements of the middle and secondary classrooms (Jackson, 1986).

While the school administration generally publishes a monthly school-wide newsletter, a beginning teacher should not make the mistake of regarding this as sufficient communication. The school-wide newsletter presents district issues and information about school activities in general. However, this does not adequately inform parents as to the specific content their students are learning in your classroom. Therefore, it is essential that you develop and maintain classroom newsletters. We recognize that middle and secondary level teachers will have multiple class preparations. However, with just a little ingenuity and pre-planning you will be able to meet the challenge. Informing parents about the curriculum and requirements in your classes will take time initially. However, the rewards of informed, supportive parents are always worth the effort. Sharing a copy of your course syllabus with parents is an important step in involving parents of older students in classroom activities.

MR. EDGAR'S ENGLISH UPDATE

Experienced middle and secondary teachers and administrators suggest that newsletters should:

- ✎ Be brief — two pages maximum.

- ✎ Be sent home at the beginning of each significant unit of study.

- ✎ Be concise but conversational, not laden with educational and content jargon.

- ✎ Review unit objectives that have been studied and link these to new units of study.

- ✎ Preview the goals and activities planned for the new units of study.

- ✎ Acknowledge any students, parents, staff and/or community members who supported the classes' instructional efforts.

- ✎ Include a parent/student signature return-response section, thus insuring that the newsletter has been received and read.

Example:

I have read and reviewed the contents of this newsletter.

Student name _____ Date _____

Parent name _____ Phone _____

Please identify any questions, suggestions, or contributions that you may have regarding the curriculum.

_____

_____

_____

News Flashes

There are times when events occur that require immediate publication. These items might range from TV coverage about your classroom activities, or students receiving school honors, or announcing the death of a classmate or teacher. News flashes are very brief, but still cover the **Who, What, Where, When** and **Why** of classroom activities.

Mr. Arns' American history students and Ms. Marks' science students have combined their talents to construct models of the greatest American inventions. The students have also written research papers about the inventors and the origin and historical impact of the invention.

The project reports and models will be displayed in the school media center during Science Week (January 10—17, 1993). Parents may view the projects on Science Fair Night, Thursday, January 14, 1993, from 6 – 9:00 P.M.

We hope to see you there.

Phone Calls

Another powerful tool for communicating with parents is the telephone. Unfortunately, phone calls are usually reserved for "bad news." Phone calls that reinforce positive student performance or behavior are a sure way to establish and build a good working relationship with parents. In either case, when you call, be sure that you have the parents' correct surname, as there are many step-families in today's schools. The example below is a way to manage and keep a record of phone conversations.

Sample Phone Call Log

Date	Child's name	Parent's name	Phone #	Regarding	Action

Beginning teachers must decide before school starts whether to share their private phone number with students. The answer may depend on your school district's policy. To assure privacy, many districts strongly recommend that teachers not disseminate private numbers to anyone but your colleagues. Other districts may vigorously encourage you to be available to parents and community members. Remember to ask the school principal or secretary if there is a standing phone number policy before you make your decision.

NOTES

Section C

Parent-Teacher Conferences

Successful conferences are the result of careful planning and organization. A successful conference means that parents and teachers have:

- ✏ Shared information about the students and both have a better understanding and appreciation of the student's needs and abilities.

- ✏ Developed a mutual trust and respect for each other and will continue to work together for the benefit of the student (Canady & Sayfarth, 1979; Jackson, 1986).

Conference Scheduling

Begin scheduling conferences *at least two weeks prior* to the first conference dates. To do this, you will need to make sure that you:

☞ Arrange conferences so that parents can attend early in the morning, shortly after school, or in the evening.

☞ Allow 15–20 minutes per conference and **do not schedule too many conferences back-to-back.**

☞ Establish first-response, first-scheduled policy.

☞ Allow a choice of three times slots in order of preference so that parents may schedule conferences at convenient times. They are more likely to attend if the schedule is established by them.

☞ Include a response confirmation sheet.

When a majority of parents have responded, **call the parents who have not responded** (we have found that this saves a great deal of frustration and paper tag). After you have scheduled everyone, publish a confirmed schedule of everyone's appointment (this seems to reaffirm the importance of everyone participating).

Post on door

Dear Parents,
      Thank you for returning the conference form. The conferences have been scheduled as follows.

Monday	Tuesday	Wednesday	Thursday
AM	AM	AM	AM
7:45 Jones	7:45 Smith		7:45 _____
8:00 Ortega	8:00 Carpenter		8:00 _____
			PM
			1:00 McAda
			1:15 Jacobs
			1:30 Padilla
			1:45 Gomez
			2:30 _____
			2:45 _____
			3:00 Walters
			3:15 Cagley
	PM		4:00 Atkinson
	4:00 Powell		4:15 _____
	4:15 McShow		4:30 Cahoe
	4:30 Fullerton		4:45 Dunsmore
	4:45 Burgess		5:00 Lindsey
	5:00 Linton		6:00 Christie
	6:00 Garcia		6:15 Kimerer
	6:15 Jefferson		6:30 Stamm
	6:30 Black		6:45 _____
	6:45 _____		

Dear Parents,

I am looking forward to talking with each of you during Parent-Teacher Conference Week, November 1 — 5. Please sign up for the three time slots which are most convenient for you. To assure you receive the time slot that is best for you, **please send in the response form as soon as possible.**

Please note that, because of Parent-Teacher Conferences, children will be released at 12:00 on Thursday and Friday, November 4th and 5th. If this creates a child-care problem, please call the school office to enroll your child, temporarily, in the after-school program.

Child's name _____ Teacher _____

Parent's name _____ Phone # _____

Place a **1, 2 and 3** by your first three choices of conference times.

Monday	Tuesday	Wednesday		Thursday
AM	AM	AM		AM
7:45____	7:45____			7:45____
8:00____	8:00____			8:00____
				PM
				1:00____
				1:15____
				1:30____
				1:45____
				2:30____
				2:45____
				3:00____
		PM		3:15____
		4:00____		4:00____
		4:15____		4:15____
		4:30____		4:30____
		4:45____		4:45____
		5:00____		5:00____
		6:00____		6:00____
		6:15____		6:15____
		6:30____		6:30____
		6:45____		6:45____

Veteran's View:
You may need to have this letter translated to another language.

Principal's Principles:
You may need to have a language translator at some conferences; contact office for suggestions.

Parents need a confirmation of date and time. Most importantly, they need some guidance about organizing their thoughts and questions about their child's progress. The following example confirmation letter is useful for just that purpose.

Sample Confirmation Letter

Dear _____,

Your conference has been scheduled for _____ at _____.

To help make the most of our time, I am sending this questionnaire to help focus our conference. Please read it and think about the answers. If you have any other questions, just write them down on this survey.

1. What is your child's favorite school subject(s)?

2. What is your child's least favorite subject(s)?

3. What do you view as your child's greatest strength(s)?

4. What area(s) are you most concerned about?

5. How is your child's overall health?

6. Are there health concerns the teacher should be aware of?

7. At home, my child most enjoys _____.

8. At home, my child least enjoys _____.

Other concerns or questions _____

_____

I am looking forward to our time together. Should any problems arise, please call the school (xxx-xxxx) as soon as possible so that we may reschedule.

Sincerely,

P.S. Remember, school will be released early on November 4th and 5th.

Super Suggestion: *Again, translation may be necessary. Begin to locate these resources early in the year.*

Portfolio Evaluation System

From the first week of school, the teacher needs to begin collecting formal and informal documentation of student progress. Experienced teachers offer these suggestions for developing and managing a portfolio evaluation system:

- Use a sturdy two-pocket folder with center tabs for sequentially organizing observational notes.

- Give each student a special number (corresponds alphabetically). Students write their name in one corner of their work, their number in the other. Using numbers in addition to names allows even kindergartners to help collate and file student work.

- Label the portfolio with the student's name and number.

- Teacher files only confidential information; students help to file all other materials.

- File all formal evaluations such as standardized test results, unit tests, district criterion referenced tests, basal placement tests, etc.

- File all informal tests. These could include reading inventories, running records, teacher made tests, etc.

- Collect and file samples of work from all content areas.

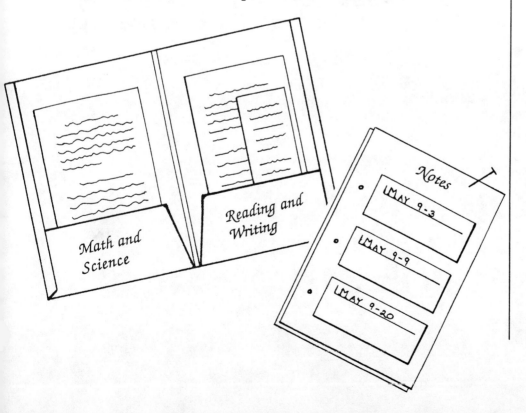

Observations and Anecdotal Notes

Standardized tests and paper-pencil products offer a narrow view of a child's capabilities. This is especially true of minority and low socioeconomic students. A unique feature of the portfolio evaluation system is the extensive use of teacher observations and anecdotal notes to help parents and other educators "see" a more complete portrait of the child's abilities and behavior in class. To help facilitate observation and anecdotal note-taking, we suggest that you:

- ☞ Use large (3 X 5) self-sticking labels and distribute several sheets of them on clipboards throughout your classroom and at your work table.
  Attach a pen to each clipboard.

- ☞ Observe children interacting with others in learning centers or in work or play groups.

- ☞ Describe (not interpret) the event as accurately as possible.

- ☞ Date each entry and identify the child you're observing.

Teachers who have practiced this observation technique find that they are able to write an anecdotal episode about each student in their classrooms about once a week. At the end of the week, the teacher collects all the written notes, peels and places them, in chronological order, in the student's portfolio.

Example:

Dawn	9/26/92
Home Center	Dramatic Play

Dawn is using her decoding skills to read the food labels. She has also shown her ability to hear beginning sounds as she writes her grocery list for the store.

A week or two prior to the conferences, review each student's portfolio. Arrange the material from the beginning of the year to the present. Make sure that the products that are included in the portfolio are an accurate representation of the child's ability. At this point you should be ready to complete the report card and the parent conference form.

Coach's Corner:
Teachers often ask, "What do I look for when I observe?" To help guide observations, use an open-ended question (one per week) that needs observations to adequately answer it. Example: "How does _____ express his/her wants and needs when working and playing with other children?"

Super Suggestion:
Take a clipboard out to the playground when you are on duty. It is a great way to learn about the whole child.

Parent Conference Format

When you are planning parent teacher conferences for the first time, we strongly recommend that you use the Parent Conference Plan. This format helps to clearly delineate both teacher and parent concerns, keeps the conference focused and purposeful, and increases the chance that the parents will view you as eager to help their child.

1. Positive statement: The teacher's first sentences establish the foundation for a proactive conference. Positive statements are sincere and usually personal.

Example: "*John* has a great sense of humor."

" *Mary* has a terrific smile."

2. Explanation of the conference steps/process: Reviewing the conference process relieves stress and actually helps to keep the conference moving in a positive direction.

- ☞ **"First,** I am going to ask you to share with me what you have observed about (name) _____ this year that makes you feel good about his/her learning? I will then ask you to discuss the concerns you have about your son's/daughter's learning."

- ☞ **"Then,** I will share some of (name) _____'s work with you and my observations about what encourages and interferes with his/her learning. We'll then discuss ideas that will continue to enhance your son/daughter's learning opportunities."

- ☞ **"Finally,** we'll summarize the conference by reviewing those things we talked about that stimulate (name) _____'s learning."

Super Suggestion: While the parents are sharing their views about their child's progress, you can write them on the Parent Conference Form. This helps parents realize how important their perceptions are to you.

3. Parent Input: It is important for parents to focus on the academic/social strengths their child possesses when they meet with you. It is also important for you to know what they view as their child's major academic concerns.

4. Teacher Input: For the continued success of the parent-teacher relationship, it is important for parents to hear about their child's academic and social strengths. Therefore, it is important when you review the student's work to highlight the positive aspects of the student's progress as much as possible.

When you begin to discuss the student's area(s) of academic/social concerns, you need to provide concrete examples or illustrations. Use the anecdotal records and work from the student's portfolio to demonstrate both areas of strength and concern. Often the issues the parents reveal are the same or related to the concerns you have. Whenever possible, connect these concerns. Again, this reinforces the feeling that you and the parents are seeking the same goals — that of helping students learn.

As you review areas of academic or social need, it is important to solicit the parents' views and suggestions and provide concrete examples for helping the student to improve.

5. Closure: To make sure both the teacher and parents have the same understanding of the content of the conference, it is necessary to briefly review with them the main ideas that were discussed during the conference. Again, using the Parent Conference Form, you may facilitate closure efforts by paraphrasing and taking notes about the discussion.

PARENT CONFERENCE FORM

Student's name _____ Parent's name _____

Conference date _____ time _____

1. Positive statement: _____

_____

2. Explanation of the conference process/steps.

3. Parent input:

What have you observed about _____ this year that makes you feel good about his/her learning?

_____

_____

_____

4. Teacher input:

I would like to share some observations about _____ that I think encourages his/her learning (concrete examples).

_____

_____

_____

5. Closure:

Let's review those things we talked about that will stimulate learning success.

_____

_____

_____

Notes:

Avoiding Conference Confrontations

Sometimes the information you must share about a student is difficult for the parents to hear. How you convey this type of information can "make or break" a conference. Negative statements may cause parents to become defensive and stop listening. Parents will more likely continue to listen if the teacher **focuses on the positive,** for example, "Joe can pass the class if ...." rather than "Joe will fail the class unless ...." The following examples provide a negative statement, then samples of more positive ways to express the same points, and examples of supporting details.

Negative Style	Positive Style	Supporting Details
He wastes half the morning fooling around.	He has so much energy and curiosity that he sometimes has trouble keeping focused on his work.	He talks to his friends; looks to see what others are doing.
When something is difficult for him, he won't even try.	He's a good worker when he's familiar with the material. He needs to apply the same habits to unfamiliar material.	When the work is difficult, he asks to leave the room, tears the paper; throws his book on the floor.
If he doesn't like you, you know it. He makes fun of children who are not in his group.	He's very perceptive; he can identify with other people's strengths as well as their weaknesses. That gives him an edge that he sometimes uses to best the other children.	He knows what makes others self-conscious (weight, height, braces), and he points it out to them (calls them fat, "shorty," "tinsel teeth").
He's disrespectful to adults.	He's very confident about his judgment. He often debates well, and in certain academic classes, that's good. But he needs to learn the limits of an appropriate debate.	He questions why he has to put a book away, to form a line for fire drill, to sit properly in his seat.
His peers tease and taunt him and make him the scapegoat.	He works hard and is very polite, but seems to have trouble gaining his classmates' respect.	The others tease him about his glasses and front teeth.

Adapted from Daine Urgban and Ruth Sammartano, Learning 89, October.

Managing Conference Confrontations

Unfortunately, even the most prepared and tactful teacher will at one time or another deal with a frustrated or hostile parent. Generally, these parents are upset because they believe that their child is not being treated fairly or given enough attention. The following scenarios (adapted from Jessica Lighter and Mary Travis, 1986) illustrate specific types of hostile behavior. **The goal in all cases is to:**

- ☛ diffuse the parent's anger/frustration, and

- ☛ begin to develop solutions to improve or resolve the problem.

Frustrated Parent To Unsuspecting Teacher:

"My daughter cries every night. The kids on the playground tease and hurt her. The teacher on duty can't make the other kids behave. I work and I can't come to school everyday to protect her."

Teacher's Verbal And Nonverbal Response:

- Listen, with ears and eyes

- Sense the parent's inner feelings

- Acknowledge the validity of the parent's concerns

"I understand. I would be upset if my daughter cried every night. I will speak to the teacher on playground duty and watch for a few days as well. After I have talked to the duty teacher and observed for a few days, let's talk on the phone again. I'll try to determine why the children are teasing your daughter, then we'll work together on finding a solution."

Hostile Parent:

"My son's math hasn't improved since he was placed with you."

Teacher's Response:

[Ignore direct "attack"; instead, focus attention on the student's problem.]

"I'm concerned about his math too. Let's focus on what we think his academic difficulties are and how we can work together to help him."

Overtly Aggressive Parent:

Occasionally a parent is so angry and verbally abusive that the present conference cannot accomplish anything constructive. At this point, the teacher needs to end the conference.

Teacher: (Standing up, concerned, calm tone of voice)

"I don't believe we can resolve these issues now. I will need to contact you to reschedule another conference when the Principal can join us."

Unreasonable hostility may have origins beyond the child's problems at school. Rescheduling the conference allows tempers to cool and time for the teacher to further investigate possible reasons for the parent's aggressive behavior.

Setting the Scene

The day of conferences has arrived. You have scheduled parents and have organized the student portfolios, completed report cards, and completed conference format forms. To complete your preparation, you will need to consider reorganizing a waiting area and consider where you will conduct the conference.

Waiting Area: On the days of the parent-teacher conferences, you will want to consider providing a waiting area for parents as even the most carefully planned schedule can go awry. Obviously, it is important that your full attention be focused on the parent(s) you are currently meeting. Therefore, if possible, the waiting area should be visually and auditorily set apart from the regular classroom.

Conference Setting: It has been noted that conducting the conference at your desk, with you sitting directly across from the parents may convey an adversarial message. To encourage positive interaction and promote two-way dialogue, we strongly suggest that you conduct the conference at a "neutral" location, such as a round or rectangular table located in a private section of the classroom.

Coach's Corner: *To keep ongoing conferences from being interrupted, post a "Conference in Session" sign.*

Veteran's View: *Remind parents that everyone has a turn and encourage patience. Post the master list of all conference times.*

Super Suggestion: *In your waiting area, include some of the products the students have created such as group reports, stories, a classroom photo album.*

Principal's Principles: *Occasionally, a parent might want to know how another student in your class is progressing. It is important for you to remember that this information is confidential.*

Super Suggestion: *Being organized is easier if you keep all student materials in portfolios and all the portfolios in a file box that is close to your conference setting.*

References

Canady, R.L., & Sayfarth, J.T. (1979). How parent-teacher conferences build partnerships. Phi Delta Kappa Educational Foundation. Bloomington, Indiana.

Jackson, P. (1986). How to build public relationships that motivate real support. NASSP Bulletin December, 25 - 31.

Lighter, Jessica & Travis, Mary (1986). article, Ways to manage hostile parents.

NOTES

Chapter 4

The Law and the Public School Teacher

Teachers are faced with making hundreds of decisions each day. The majority of instructional decisions are planned and purposeful. However, the management of students, contacts with parents, and the interplay of teachers' personal and professional lives frequently demand prudent judgment and reason.

To avoid unfortunate incidents that could result in litigation, teachers must be aware of the laws that protect them and their students.

This chapter will summarize ten areas of school law that will assist teachers with responsibly assuming classroom teaching assignments.

Pay Attention to Your Legal "Do's"

1. Recognize the implications of separation of church and state and avoid worshiping in public school classrooms.

2. Understand the influence you may have on students with regard to politics, current events, etc. to avoid abusing academic freedom. Use prudent judgment when publicly criticizing school policies or personnel.

3. Understand the relationship between your private activities, such as lifestyle preference or consumption of alcohol, and your employment as a teacher. Recognize that your private activities can be perceived as influencing your abilities or effectiveness as a teacher.

4. Understand the copyright law. You may make duplicated copies of materials as long as the copies do not violate the fair use doctrine. Four criteria dictate your authority to make copies of an author's copyrighted work without first securing permission:

   ✔ The purpose and character of the use

   ✔ The nature of the copyrighted work

   ✔ The amount and portion of the work copied

   ✔ The effect of the use upon the potential market

Principal's Principles: Teachers are viewed as minor celebrities by the students and their parents. When shopping or socializing in the community where you teach, remember to maintain your teacher persona.

Super Suggestion: Should you have doubt about duplicates of a document (written, audio, and/or video), check with the school librarian for guidance.

5. Recognize that students must be afforded due process for offenses that may result in suspension or expulsion.

6. Understand the state statutes on the administration of corporal punishment to students. Moreover, be aware of district/school policies that permit or deny the use of corporal punishment.

7. Avoid ridiculing students in classrooms or discussing students in teachers' lounges, so as to not be perceived as slandering students. Avoid sharing personal, derogatory files concerning students that could be misconstrued as libel.

8. Recognize your responsibilities to protect the safety of your students. Teachers must use due care and must avoid carelessness lest it lead to injury. Content area teachers such as physical education teachers, science teachers, or industrial arts teachers who, by the nature of the content of their courses, expose students to physical risk, must exercise due care to avoid injury of students.

9. Avoid punishing students for behavioral problems through academic penalties. For example, teachers should not award a student a lower grade for a course/subject than he/she has earned because of poor behavior.

10. Know your rights as teachers and recognize the responsibilities that accompany those rights!

Chapter 5

The "Magic" of Student Management

Section A:

Matching Philosophies

Packaged Discipline Plans

Age-Appropriate Techniques

Section B:

Parent Involvement

Believe in the Magic:
   Teachers Talking To Teachers

Section A

Beginning teachers leave teacher preparation programs armed with an arsenal of theories about how students learn, what they should learn, and how students should behave so that they can learn. Yet, many beginning teachers report inordinate frustration and anxiety regarding the actual or anticipated behavior of their students as well as their own lack of self-confidence and skill in the management of student behavior. Knowing about student discipline techniques and implementing them can seem to be wholly unrelated notions, particularly when beginners are barraged with the overwhelming scope of responsibilities faced by teachers new to the classroom.

There is little doubt that the challenge of effectively managing student behavior in the classroom has grown in proportion to the social and family problems created by poverty, substance abuse, unemployment, and so forth. Yet, in spite of increasingly challenging circumstances, effective teachers do create rich, safe learning environments almost as if by magic. Anyone, trained or untrained, can walk into a classroom and sense whether the teacher is in control. Often, that perception translates to judgments about the teacher's ability to control students. In the strictest sense, few, if any, of us can absolutely control another's behavior. What productive teachers can do is establish a context for learning, a setting in which students know, understand, and practice behavioral expectations within clearly defined boundaries. Maintaining a well-managed classroom is not about control. Rather, it is about carefully preparing an environment that is warm, caring, safe, and stimulating. If students know and can demonstrate the behaviors that will be tolerated, and if the identified consequences for intolerable behavior are swiftly and uniformly applied, beginning teachers can efficiently manage student behavior with the seeming magic of the practiced veteran.

Matching Philosophies
(Are you in the right school for you?)

Beginning teachers are hired because they meet the criteria for employment established by an interview team. Typically, student discipline issues are discussed during an interview. The employment interview is the ideal time for a beginning teacher to find out about the school's policies and procedures regarding student discipline. If neglected until after a contract has been signed, new teachers may find it more difficult to align their personal philosophies with those of their new colleagues. The following questions can help you determine if you and the school are a good match.

- ✔ How may I obtain a copy of the discipline policy?

- ✔ Is there flexibility in how I implement the policy?

- ✔ What are the most frequent types of student discipline problems in this school?

- ✔ Are teachers' actions generally supported by the administration?

- ✔ Are teachers' actions generally supported by parents?

- ✔ Do teachers work together to implement the policy?

- ✔ Is there a system-wide program/philosophy in place?

- ✔ Is a specific system of documentation of student discipline actions/referrals required?

Packaged Discipline Plans

Schools and school districts have been attracted to packaged discipline programs during the last decade. The authors' purpose is not to weigh the relative merits of these kinds of programs as much as to stress the importance of knowing if a program is in place and the expectations of teachers for compliance. If a new teacher philosophically cannot live with the expectations of a system-wide discipline program in which there is no room for modification, then the demands of teaching in such a setting will be difficult and the novice teacher will be predictably unsuccessful.

The more likely scenario is one that includes some flexibility. Even within the confines of a structured program, teachers frequently have the discretion to adapt their own styles and techniques. For example, within the Assertive Discipline program, teachers can choose to develop age-appropriate classroom rules and consequences with their students.

> **Coach's Corner:**
> Beginning teachers should assess the rigidity of the school's discipline policies before assuming responsibility for a classroom.

Some schools, particularly secondary schools, will publish lists of offenses with a range of acceptable consequences. Teachers then have the freedom to establish the "how to's" within their classrooms. Other schools may recommend specific books or journal articles that offer a proposed discipline structure or philosophy. Regardless of the setting or grade level, it is likely that a student discipline policy exists. It is the beginning teacher's responsibility to find out what are the standards for behavior and the established discipline plan. This information can best be obtained from the school principal.

Age-Appropriate Techniques

Discipline strategies can vary as much with students' age, interests, development, and family history as with the unique styles of teachers.

Young Children: Generally, the environment created for young children accounts for their growth and development. Therefore, the behavior of young children is guided and shaped rather than ruled and disciplined. Placing kindergartners' and first graders' names on the board with accompanying check-marks for inappropriate behavior usually becomes a meaningless and frustrating effort. A child-centered classroom for young children that provides for decision-making, large blocks of time allocated for play, and learning centers strategically located throughout the room also allows young children to argue and negotiate, to freely express themselves verbally and creatively, and to openly choose activities of interest. Beginning teachers of young children are faced more with organizational challenges than procedural issues. For example, learning centers are organized so that they accommodate natural traffic patterns, minimize noise in quiet areas, and maximize opportunities for social interaction and play. Thereby, a variety of appropriate student behaviors is anticipated and acceptable.

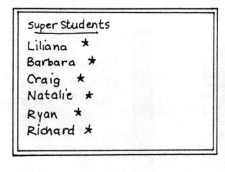

Older Students: Beginning teachers of older students process, develop, and thoroughly discuss rules and consequences with the students. Rules of thumb include:

✔ Identify a manageable number of classroom rules. (No more than 5!)

✔ Keep rules and consequences simple.

✔ Teach the rules; model the behaviors; rehearse the procedures; practice the behaviors.

✔ Reinforce the rules uniformly and fairly.

✔ Apply the consequences consistently and immediately.

✔ Routinely inform parents about both appropriate and inappropriate behavior.

✔ Focus on the process of establishing procedures at the outset of the school year and practice until they are automatic for both you and the students. Curriculum content can wait!

Tip for teachers of secondary students:

✔ Include the management plan developed with students in the course syllabus and send a copy home to parents.

Principal's Principles: Have the principal review your discipline plan and the parent note that explains your classroom policies and procedures.

Super Suggestion: Include a parent signature/return form with your discipline/manage plan.

Section B

Parent Involvement

Inherent in the success of a beginning teacher at any grade level is frequent, scheduled contact with parents. There has been considerable publicity recently about the value of involving parents in their children's education. Yet, veteran teachers have known for years that their success is largely dependent on the extent of their efforts to team with parents to provide educational opportunities. The family structure of the 90's is not always conducive to active involvement by parents with schools. Nonetheless, the effort must be extended. Data indicate that parents of younger children are more involved than parents of older students. The waning of parental interest over time may lie as much with the expectations of teachers as with the lifestyles of parents. Most parents, regardless of their family constellations, want to know about their children's progress and behavior in school at every grade level!

Schools traditionally schedule a number of forums for parent participation, i.e. Open House, parent-teacher conferences, fund-raising activities. These are ideal opportunities to communicate with parents about behavior and academic progress. More important, however, than the formal meetings are the casual conversations designed for both informing and listening. Teachers should contact parents by phone or in person within the first three weeks of the start of school. The purposes of the contact are to introduce yourself, to gather helpful information about students and families, and to briefly comment about positive, and if necessary, inappropriate behaviors. The power of these initial contacts is untold. Establishing a relationship with parents guarantees big payoffs for both teacher and student throughout the school year. The challenge then becomes to maintain frequent, informal contact with parents over the course of the year. Once teachers have established that they are caring and committed to an ongoing partnership, they have greatly increased the likelihood that parents will support them, particularly if a problem arises.

Coach's Corner:

✔ Establish a mutually convenient time to chat with parents on a regularly scheduled basis.

✔ To ensure your safety, conduct home visits with a colleague.

✔ If parents don't seem readily available or willing to talk with you on a regular basis, ask if there is an older sibling or grandparent with whom you might speak.

✔ Contact parents for positive reasons as frequently as you contact them to report negative behavior.

✔ Inquire at the outset of the school year about the feasibility of contacting parents at work.

✔ Document each contact with parents in a calendar of events or on a specially devised form.

✔ Communicate with parents through newsletters as well as through personal contact. Have a colleague or friend proofread communiques to ensure that you've said what you intended and to guard against technical errors.

✔ Uphold complete confidentiality regarding all matters discussed with parents.

Believe in the "Magic:"
Teachers Talking to Teachers

Beginning teachers are charged with the task of designing a complex mosaic of effective instructional delivery appropriately aligned with curriculum and assessment. The underpinnings consist of a useful classroom management plan of which student management is one piece.

Effective student management occurs when teachers can demonstrate that what they are doing is healthy for the learning of students. Discussing plans and activities with colleagues helps to de-mystify student management. Through honest interaction with peers, beginning teachers can build self-confidence, reduce anxiety, and create that seemingly "magical" rapport with students. Knowing about and implementing effective student discipline strategies are integrally related. Understanding, believing in, and affirming the formula for success, help beginning teachers to implement all that they have learned about student management.

Coach's Corner:

✔ Teachers must UNDERSTAND that preparing the classroom environment so that it is age- and content-appropriate will ensure the success of student discipline strategies.

✔ Teachers must BELIEVE in their overall plan for student management.

✔ Teachers must AFFIRM their practices with their colleagues.

Chapter 6

Juggling, Balancing, and Spinning.....
Or Ways to Manage Stress

Stress and the Beginning Teacher

Creating a Comfortable Work Environment

Recognizing and Relieving Stress

Ways to Manage Stress

Balance

Stress and the Beginning Teacher

The life of a teacher is hectic. All teachers have district demands, "ASAP" office requests, a mile-high stack of paperwork, and a dozen student crises all requiring attention—right now! Welcome to the juggling and balancing act called the teaching profession. Even though this may be a "normal" way of life, it can be particularly stressful for the beginner. The purpose of this chapter is to discuss ways to:

✔ Make the work environment more comfortable

✔ Recognize and relieve stress

✔ Balance work and play

Creating a Comfortable Work Environment

The first day is rapidly approaching and you are busily, maybe even frantically, preparing to meet your students. This is an exciting, stressful time for all teachers, but more so for beginners. As you prepare your room to be an exciting learning environment, we strongly recommend you also take some time to create a comfortable work environment for yourself.

Coach's Corner:

✔ Bring a small, electric, hot-water pot to school so you can make coffee, tea, hot cocoa or soup during your breaks or after school. (Check district policy first!)

✔ Keep a supply of storable, high protein/carbohydrate snacks to consume when your energy level runs low.

✔ Bring a radio/tape player. Enjoy listening to your favorite music when you are planning your lessons.

✔ Bring an extra sweater, umbrella, and a comfortable pair of shoes; keep in your closet or desk drawer. You never know when you might need extra comfort or warmth.

✔ Hang a mirror in your room. Keep extra grooming supplies in your desk.

✔ Bring tissues and it never hurts to have a bottle of pain relievers.

✔ Buy an adhesive-backed hook. Put it on your classroom door. Place your keys and whistle there.

Recognizing and Relieving Stress

As mentioned previously, teaching is rewarding, challenging, and fulfilling, but at the same time it is demanding, energy-draining and time-consuming. Becoming a teacher, just like being a newcomer in any other professional career, will require many adjustments. New faces, new responsibilities, new surroundings.... all of these things together will often cause a sense of being "stressed." Symptoms frequently associated with stress include:

- Recurring headaches

- Laryngitis

- Stomach problems

- Frequent heartburn

- Hostile feelings/language

- Sudden outbursts of anger

- Depression/crying

- Sudden weight changes

- Tense or cramped back/neck muscles

If you are experiencing any of these symptoms, or any combination of these symptoms, it is important that you seek a doctor's attention. Mental/physical stress symptoms are your body's way of telling you to take it easy and put some balance back into your life. Remember, a "stressed-out" teacher does not help anyone.

Ways To Manage Stress

1. **Set working goals for yourself.** Career Track specialists Calano and Salzman (1991), suggest that these goals be SMART.

   S = specific,
   M = measurable,
   A = attainable,
   R = realistic, and allow enough
   T = time to accomplish them.

2. **Create a list of goals every day and prioritize them.** To keep yourself goal-focused and on track, refer to your list throughout the day. You will be amazed at the sense of satisfaction you feel when you cross off the task/goals you have accomplished.

3. **Laugh daily.** Plan fun in your lessons; it will make teaching and learning more enjoyable for you and your students.

4. **Take care of yourself.** Take vitamins, eat a nutritious diet, exercise, and arrange your schedule so that you can get 6–8 hours of sleep a night.

5. **Develop a support system.** Talk to positive veteran teachers or a mentor teacher. Share your frustrations and your triumphs. Take a 20-minute rest break after your students leave. Enjoy a snack and a beverage. Relax and talk to your colleagues. Sharing ideas and concerns with experienced peers is always helpful, stimulating, and reassuring.

6. **Join a professional organization.** Attend workshops and conferences; networking with other professionals is invigorating. Reading professional journals can give you many new ideas on how to solve instructional problems or create new learning opportunities for your students.

7. **Separate home time from school time.** Bringing school work home only adds to your working day. Instead, use your time at school wisely. Stay until you finish grading today's work and have prepared for tomorrow's lessons. Then when you go home, you won't be worried about when you will have time to finish your school work. (For more suggestions, see Chapter 2 "Putting It Together for the First Time").

8. **When you are ill, stay home.** Trying to teach when you are sick only prolongs the illness and wears you down further. The next chapter provides specific information about preparing for a substitute teacher. One of the best stress relievers is being prepared for absences.

Mentor's Memo:
The "F" word in education is FLEXIBILITY. Learning to "roll with the flow" is critical. Laughing at the broken bell system that rings every other minute all day long is much healthier than becoming frustrated or angry. If you think of it as adventure in schooling, your students will too.

Balance

Do you have hobbies? Family and friends? Though highly fulfilling, teaching is also intense. You were not hired to be a teacher 24 hours each day. To avoid "burn-out" and to continue to enjoy your life, it is important for you to set aside time for activities that ease mental, emotional, and physical stress. Successful, experienced teachers advise beginning teachers to find a balance of personal and professional activities and never feel guilty about spending time for yourself.

Chapter 7

Yes, You Will Get Sick:
Preparing for the Substitute Teacher

Section A:

How To Make A Substitute Teacher Happy

Section B:

How To Be A Successful Substitute Teacher

Surviving as a Substitute

Learning While You Substitute

References

Section A

How To Make A Substitute Teacher Happy

Even if you have "not had a cold in years," the likelihood of beginning teachers needing the services of a substitute teacher is very high (it takes time to build natural immunities). Therefore, the authors strongly recommend that as soon as you have established a consistent daily schedule, you should organize a SUBSTITUTE FOLDER. The goal of developing a substitute folder is to help the substitute teacher provide a coherent, quality educational experience during your absence.

A simple way to organize a substitute folder is to label a two pocket folder with center tabs to hold lists and memos. Inside the folder, we suggest you include the following:

Lists:

- a current seating plan of your class(es)
- students who attend special classes and the times they leave the classroom
- a list of bus riders or walkers
- a skeleton outline of your daily schedule
- a timeline of the school's schedule
- list of ability/interest groups
- names of students who are helpful
- names of students who need special attention
- names of teachers that will be helpful
- your home phone number, in case of an emergency

Procedures:

- details regarding your welcoming/opening routines
- directions concerning your attendance procedures
- details concerning your management/discipline system
- information concerning specific instructional procedures
- bathroom routines
- details regarding any duties to which you are assigned

Directions:

- location of supplies and instructional materials
- school map
- location of special classes
- location of teachers' workroom/restroom

Emergency Procedures:

- directions for fire drill.
- disruptive behavior protocol
- severe weather/rainy day schedule

Forms:

Include blank forms for

- discipline referral
- hall pass
- library pass
- Nurse's Office pass
- Guidance/Counselor Office pass

Who's Who:

Names and school phone extensions of:

- Principal
- Assistant Principal
- Guidance Counselor
- Secretary
- Nurse
- Custodian

Example of Substitute Folder:

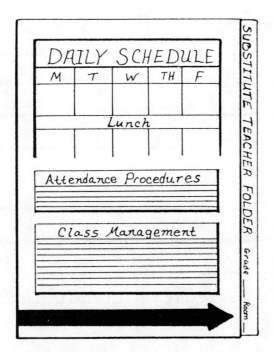

Include a Substitute Teacher's Evaluation form in your folder.

Example:

Substitute Teacher's Name _____ Date _____

Phone # _____

Overall evaluation of student behavior:

Disorderly/Rude   Cooperative/Polite

1   2   3   4   5   6   7   8

Individuals who were highly supportive/well behaved:

_____

_____

Individuals who were uncooperative/poorly behaved:

_____

_____

Please list any assignments you were unable to complete:

_____

_____

Other comments:

_____

_____

_____

Please attach the homework you collected to this form.

Thank you.

Principal's Principles:
Many districts will ask you to evaluate the substitute teacher's performance. This information is used to determine who will be rehired to substitute at the school again. By that same token, the substitute may also be asked to evaluate your efforts to prepare for a substitute teacher.

Super Suggestion:
At the end of each day, prepare for the eventuality of a substitute the following day. Collect and organize all instructional materials. Place them and the SUB FOLDER on top of your desk. That way, you are always ready for tomorrow, no matter what happens.

Veteran's View:
*Districts have policies and procedures regarding substitute teachers. Read your district handbook to determine:
* whom you call to request a substitute,
* if you can specify a particular individual, and
* to whom do substitute teachers report.*

Super Suggestion:
When the district determines who will substitute for you, ask them to give the substitute your home phone number. When the sub calls, you can relate any additional information that will help the substitute teach your class successfully.

Section B

How To Be A Successful Substitute Teacher

If you can't find a teaching position, one way to establish yourself as an excellent candidate is to work as a substitute teacher. To apply for a substitute teaching position, contact the district personnel office. Districts use similar hiring procedures to employ substitutes; therefore, you may wish to use the suggestions detailed in Chapter One.

To increase your chances of being called to substitute, you may need to make contacts in numerous districts. Joining local teacher associations is one way to begin making connections. Another is to make an appointment to meet the principal or assistant principal at the schools where you wish to substitute (ask the secretary to make the appointment with whomever is in charge of working with substitutes). When you meet with the appropriate administrator, be warm and friendly, bring your portfolio, and share your career goals. Within a short time, you will receive calls to work as a substitute teacher.

Surviving as a Substitute

The first rule of subbing is be prepared!

- When you get "the call", it may be in the wee hours of the morning. Keep a memo pad and pencil by your phone. Find out as much as possible about the grade/subjects and school. Ask if you may call the teacher.

- Call the teacher! Ask about the location of lesson plan book and any other information he/she may wish to tell you.

- Use a briefcase or large bag/backpack to bring extra supplies/materials you may need. (Normal pacing is sometimes accelerated as students are often excited when the normal routine changes).

- Bring supplies for a simple, but exciting art activity for primary or intermediate grades.

- Bring literature stories that are fun and interesting.

- Include brain-teasers or mind expanders for secondary students.

- Bring your own cup and a high-energy snack.

- We recommend that, unless there is no discernible discipline plan, that you, as much as possible, use the teacher's established classroom management system.

- After school, go to the teachers' lounge and introduce yourself to the other teachers. Let them know you are interested in substituting for them in the future.

- Caution—do not share any negative details about the classrooms of teachers for whom you substitute, even if other teachers ask leading questions. You don't want to earn a reputation of being a "tattletale."

Learning While You Substitute

Use the time you substitute as an opportunity to collect great teaching ideas.

✔ Bring a camera and take snapshots of creative bulletin boards.

✔ Bring a memo pad and write down examples of the best classroom management systems.

✔ Make notes of interesting math, science, and social studies activities.

✔ Call the teacher and ask him/her more about the ideas you were able to collect.

Veteran's View: *Complete any form the classroom teacher has left for you. If there is no form, write a brief memo about the students' progress.*

References

Cawthorne, B. (1987) *Instant Success for new and substitute teachers.* Greenfield Publications. Arizona, Scottsdale.

Williamson, B. (1988). *A first year teacher's guide for success: A step-by-step educational recipe book.* Dynamic Teaching Company. California, Sacramento.

Chapter 8

Teaching in Culturally and Linguistically Diverse Classrooms and Communitites

Christian J. Faltis, Arizona State University

Section A:

Expect to Have English Learners in Your classroom.

What kinds of special instructional programs have English learners had before they entered your classroom?

- Transitional Bilingual Education

- Self-contained Immersion Programs

- Sheltered English Programs

- Pull-out English ESL Programs

Who is eligible for bilingual education?

How is language proficiency assessed?

- Language assessment scales

Caution: A word about labels

Section B:

What can we do to help ESL students join in our classroom?

Section C:

What about involving parents who don't speak English?

Section A

Expect to Have English Learners in Your Classroom

The chances are great that you will teach in a classroom where at least some of the students are learning English as a second language (ESL). This is because the population of students aged 5-17 for whom English is a second language is estimated to be between 2.6 and 3.0 million nationwide.

Nationwide, the second largest population of school-age ESL learners comes from Asian and Indo-Chinese immigrant families; for example, Chinese from Taiwan, Hong Kong and more recently, mainland China; Korean; Filipino; Vietnamese; Cambodian; Khmer, Hmong; and Laotian. Large numbers of Asian-and Indo-Chinese-origin families began entering the U.S. in the 1960s. In 1980, three out of every five persons who identified themselves as Asian or Pacific Islander were born abroad. The children of these two groups, virtually all of whom were born in this country, make up the remaining two fifths. A majority of these children are reared though the native language of their parents and caregivers, and consequently enter school with little or no proficiency in English.

What Kinds of Special Instructional Programs Have English Learners Had Before They Entered Your Classroom?

Major Program Types for English Learners

1. Transitional Bilingual Education: Early-and Late-Exit Programs

2. Self-Contained Structured Immersion Programs

3. Sheltered English Programs

4. Pull-Out English as a Second Language Program

> It is predicted that the number of Spanish-speaking school-age children will increase from approximately 10 million in 1990 to 18.6 million in 2020.

> In the Southwest, Spanish-speaking children are the largest and fastest growing school-age population of ESL learners.

> In 1980, three out of every five persons who identified themselves as Asian or Pacific Islander were born abroad.

1. Transitional Bilingual Education

Many of the students that you may have in class who are still learning English probably have been in some form of a *bilingual education* program before coming to your classroom. In the United States, bilingual education has many meanings. A primary distinction is whether bilingual education leads to *additive* or *subtractive* bilingualism. Additive bilingualism is the result of programs that use the student's native language for language arts, literacy, and subject matter instruction, along with English instruction for most of student's schooling experience.

An important goal of additive bilingual education programs is to ensure that students develop high levels of proficiency in English and the student's native language. Subtractive bilingualism, in contrast, results from programs that provide relatively little or no instruction in the student's native language. In this case, the goal is to enhance English oral and literacy abilities without developing the student's native language in the process. In other words, the student's native language is replaced with English.

The overwhelming majority of bilingual education programs throughout the U.S. lead to subtractive bilingualism. Subtractive bilingual programs are designed to transition students from their native language to English as quickly as possible. The most commonly practiced subtractive educational program is called *transitional bilingual education*. This kind of program uses the native language for some or all subject matter instruction on average for no more than three academic years, while the students are learning English as a second language.

There are *early-exit* and *late-exit* bilingual programs. Students in early-exit programs are provided some kind of instruction in their native language, usually reading and language arts, for up to two years. They may, however, continue to receive English instruction on a pull-out basis for one to two class periods when they are placed in an all-English classroom. In late-exit programs, students continue having native language instruction from three to five years. Students generally stay in late-exit programs until they have learned enough English to succeed academically in an all-English classroom.

Certified teachers in both types of bilingual education programs have a special endorsement in Bilingual Instruction.

2. Self-containment

A less common type of subtractive bilingual program is called *structured immersion,* modeled after the Canadian French immersion programs designed for middle class English-speaking students in Quebec. In the U.S., structured immersion students are taught entirely in English the same subject matter content as their native English proficient counterparts in regular classrooms. Structured immersion teachers adjust their vocabulary, discourse and pacing to enhance comprehension so that students can understand the material and participate in classroom activities. The teachers are often bilingual, but avoid using the students' native language in class. Native language use among students is tolerated initially, but students are openly encouraged to use English for classroom interaction.

3. Sheltered English Programs

These programs are a relatively new form of ESL instruction for the upper elementary and secondary grades to present subject matter content through meaningful input, all in English. In sheltered English classes, English is not taught to students in terms of grammatical rules to be learned in isolation from meaning. Rather, sheltered English classes integrate language learning with content instruction. English learners are taught subject matter content (e.g., math, science, social studies, health) through comprehension-based teaching strategies. Sheltered English teachers adapt instruction by using gestures, visual aids, and certain kinds of language adjustments. They also frequently use thematic unit planning and small group learning activities to promote meaningful interaction.

Transitional bilingual education is practiced mainly in schools serving large numbers of English learners who speak and understand the same native language; for example, Spanish, Navajo or Chinese. In schools where there are English learners who speak and understand different native languages, students are assigned to structured immersion English classrooms, sheltered English classrooms, or in many cases, to ESL *pull-out* programs.

To become certified to teach in BLE programs, additional semester credit hours of coursework in bilingual education beyond certification and oral and written proficiency in the native language of instruction are required for the endorsement.

4. ESL pull-out programs

These programs are considered a form of bilingual education, but; in fact, the student's native language is rarely used for instruction. In ESL pull-out programs, second language students leave their all-English classroom at certain times during the day to receive instruction in English as a second language in a separate classroom.

Who is Eligible for Bilingual Education?

Federal and state law has made the identification of students whose primary language is not English and the evaluation of their English language proficiency mandatory in all school districts that serve bilingual communities. The first step that schools take in determining program eligibility is to identify students whose first language is not English. Most school districts in multilingual cities administer a survey to all parents when they enroll their children in school. The survey asks the following four questions?

What is your child's first language if it is a language other then English?

Is a language other than English spoken in the home?

Is the language most often spoken by your child a language other than English?

Do you speak a language other than English to your child most of the time?

An answer of "yes" to any of these questions by parents indicates that the student's primary home language is other than English. Once this has been determined, the next step is to find out whether the student has limited English proficiency, and thus, whether he or she is eligible for bilingual or ESL instructi

How is Language Proficiency Assessed?

The criteria for entering a bilingual program vary from state to state, but most states determine entry eligibility on the basis of oral English proficiency scores, English reading test scores, and native language reading test scores. The three most popular oral English language proficiency tests are the Language Assessment Scales (LAS), the Bilingual Syntax Measure (BSM), and the Individualized Developmental English Activities (IDEA) Placement Test, also referred to as the IPT. Other frequently used tests are the Basic Inventory of Natural Language (BINL) and the Language Assessment Battery (LAB). The most commonly used English reading tests are the Comprehensive Test of Basic Skills (CTBS) and the California Achievement Test (CAT). For assessing Spanish oral and literacy skills, schools most often use the Spanish version of the LAS and the Spanish version of the BSM.

To get an idea of what English proficiency tests measure, and how they distinguish levels of language proficiency, here is a brief description of the LAS test and how it works.

The Language Assessment Scales

The LAS test measures oral language skills based on a student's performance on four linguistic subsystems: the sound system, vocabulary knowledge, syntax (word order in a sentence), and pragmatics (the ability to complete certain conversational tasks in the language). The sound system is assessed by having students tell whether minimal pairs of words sound the same or sound different (30 items), and by having them repeat certain sounds of the language (36 items). Knowledge of vocabulary is tested by having students name the item in a picture (20 items). Syntax is measured through two means: oral comprehension and oral production of a story presented on an audio-cassette tape. The assessment of pragmatic ability is optional. It consists of 10 questions that draw out a student's ability to use language for describing and narrating without the use of visual story props.

Students are assigned to one of five proficiency levels on the basis of their total correct responses, which are weighted across the four subsystems. The five proficiency levels are as follows:

5 — Fully English Proficient, Highly Articulate (FEP)

4 — Fully English Proficient (FEP)

3 — Limited English Proficient (LEP)

2 — Non English Proficient; Isolated Language Ability (NEP)

1 — Non English Proficient (NEP)

Try to refer to students who are learning English as English learners or second language learners. Avoid terms that reflect negative connotations.

Students scoring in levels one and two are designated as Non English Proficient or NEPs. These students may also referred to as *monolinguals,* meaning that they are proficient in a language other than English. Level three students are called LEP students. The term LEP is often used in a more generic sense to refer to English learners without regard to their level of proficiency in English. Students at levels four and five are fully English proficient and highly articulate speakers of English.

Limited English proficient students are also sometimes referred to as "language minority students." However, this term is not necessarily restricted to English learners. It may also refer to native English speaking students who belong to an under-represented ethnic minority group, within which some of the members speak a language other than English.

Caution: A Word about Labels

You may occasionally come across the labels NES and LES, which mean non-English speaking and limited-English speaking, respectively. These labels are no longer used by educators because they are not tied to any of the major language assessment tests, and they focus rather narrowly on only one of the language skills, speaking.

Many educators prefer other ways of referring to students who are in the process of learning English as a second language. The prefixes "non-" and "limited" conjure up images children who are deficit in an important academic learning tool. Calling a student a LEP or NEP presents a negative connotation. There are many educators who prefer a more neutral term such as "English learner" or "second language learner." Admittedly, these labels also have limitations, but they do avoid some of the negative connotations associated with being limited in something that is valued in school.

Section B

What Can We Do to Help ESL Students Join in Our Classrooms?

There is no simple answer to this question. Learning to teach in a classroom where all of the students are native speakers of English is difficult already. There are some general principles, however, that you can follow when you have ESL students in your classrooms. You should constantly be on the lookout for workshops, coursework, and professional readings that address the needs of English learners in the all-English classroom. This will help you build your knowledge base and increase your teaching repertoire. In the meantime, however, you can consider the following suggestions:

1. Try to make classroom language understandable by adapting the way you explain concepts, give directions, and interact with students. Pay attention to the vocabulary and concepts that you use when you plan and implement the lesson. Move from concrete to abstract ideas and tasks. Use visual aids, such as pictures, drawings, and photographs to support meaning. Infuse gestures and physical movements into your teaching. Let students know where you are in the lesson by pointing out the major phases of the lesson: introduction, practice, and ending.

2. To the extent possible, incorporate your ESL students' native languages into bulletin boards, invitations to parents, and newsletters. Allow students to use their native language during recess and on playgrounds. They will switch to English as the language of play when they are ready. Don't worry about them learning English, all of them will; instead concern yourself with ways to support the students' native language.

3. Learn about and bring ESL students' home culture experiences into classroom activities. Whenever possible, draw on ESL students' language and cultural experiences to facilitate language and content learning. Encourage ESL students to tie in their prior experiences for making sense of classroom materials. If possible, organize theme-based activities that encourage students to exchange ideas that matter to them with and to write authentically to and for multiple audiences.

4. Vary your teaching activities to include whole group, small group and individual learning. Encourage students to engage in multiple ways of interacting with classroom materials and their peers. Never exclude ESL students from classroom or school activities. Do lots of team building and class building to encourage all students, regardless of their English proficiency, to work and talk together interdependently.

5. Learn to negotiate meaning with ESL students and model this for all of your students. Notice how you interact with your students. If you don't understand what an ESL student is trying to say to you or to the class, ask for clarification. Practice rephrasing your questions. As needed, ask ESL students to repeat their ideas and then confirm that you have understood their meaning.

6. Look for new ways to assess ESL students' knowledge of English and of subject matter. Watch how the English learners work and interact in different classroom settings with different students. Evaluate language use and literacy achievement holistically rather than as the mastery of separate skills.

Section C

What about Involving Parents Who Don't Speak English?

One of the most frustrating problems that you will face is how to interact with and involve parents who don't speak English well and who are not yet comfortable participating in school activities. This is a complicated problem with no easy solutions. Part of the solution, though, comes from taking a strong stance that you can include English learners and their families in the schooling process.

Building bridges between the home and the school rests upon the cooperative efforts between you and parents. But, you have the primary responsibility for initially getting ESL parents involved in schooling matters. The key to involving ESL parents is to strike a balance between learning about the home environments of your students, while the parents of your students also learn about school-oriented activities and programs.

You can work toward this balance of involvement by dividing the process of building bridges between the home and the school into four levels, beginning with you learning about the parents' community support systems and about stress factors related to living in a new environment and progress to having the parents actively contributing to curricular decisions. The four levels are as follows:

Level I

Your primary goals at this level are to establish contact with parents, to begin learning about their community, and to let parents know that you are there for them and that you will continue to support them throughout the school year. As you gain the trust of parents, you can begin suggesting ways to monitor schoolwork assignments completed in the home. You will increase the likelihood of getting parents involved in their child's school-work to the extent that your suggestions take into account the contraints under which the family operates. If you do not speak the language of the parents, you will need to work with a bilingual liaison to assist you in your communication with parents. (See chapter 3 in this book for more specific details.)

Level II

The second level of involvement broadens the kinds of communication that you have with parents. From your perspective, Level II involves informing parents through written sources, telephone calls, and informal conferences about their child's progress, about classroom activities that may involve their community, about upcoming events, and about basic school policies. From the parent's perspective, the communication might range from providing you with feedback on how the child is responding to schoolwork at home to inquiring about holidays and bus routes. Parents should begin to sense that school is not such a foreign place as they might have thought.

Level III

You can begin to invite parents to participate in your classroom and in school-related activities as soon as you sense that parents and family members are responding favorably to your efforts to contact and inform them of schooling and community-related activities. Your primary objective in Level III is to get parents into the classroom to informally observe and eventually help with classroom activities and school events. At the same time, with your guidance, you also want parents to take on increasing responsibility for monitoring their child's study skills and work habits at home. In essence, you want the parents' experiences in school to serve as a model for the kinds of support and monitoring that they can provide for their children at home.

It is important to understand that while you may have contact with 100 percent of your ESL parents as a result of your efforts in Levels I and II, in all probability, there will be some parents who may resist becoming involved at this level for any number of reasons.

One way of involving parents who are able to help in the classroom is to have certain parents contribute to making bulletin boards and other kinds of decorations and building projects. For example, if you decorate your classroom around thematic units and festivities, parents can help you put up bulletin boards. You can set aside several locations in your classroom for non-English language bulletin boards. Parents can also help in the preparation of classroom materials. They can come into the classroom to work on assembling a stage for a classroom play, or they can sew and cut materials for a cooperative game. ESL parents will participate in your classroom and in school in many ways when they start to feel that the school is a comfortable place to be and that it is potentially a resource for them.

Level IV

In this fourth and highest level of parental and teacher involvement, the goal is to enable parents to play an more decisive role in school decisions and policies, and at the same time to increase the level of confidence and trust that parents have in you as the teacher. To achieve this highest level of involvement, you and the parents must have experienced each of the first three levels. Accordingly, Level IV is clearly not for every parent, and in fact, few parents attain it. Those ESL parents who do reach Level IV often become community spokespersons to whom you can look to for both advice and support. Accordingly, you can ask for their opinions on classroom ideas, and as their participation progresses, for their advise on curriculur decisions at the school level.

As you can see, there are many ways to involve parents regardless of their proficiency in English. The key to parental involvement with ESL families to learn as much as you can about the families and their communities and to plan their involvement in phases, understanding that not all parents need to participate at all levels.

During your student teaching experience, talk with your cooperating teacher about how he or she works to involve ESL parents. If possible talk with other teachers throughout your experience. Let other teachers know that you are interested in helping ESL students participate fully in your classroom. Listen to their concerns and to their advice.

Chapter 9

Working with Special Needs Children in the Regular Classroom Mainstream

Samuel A. DiGangi, Arizona State University

Section A:

Least Restrictive Environment

Section B:

Limitations of Categorical Labels

Section C:

Questions about Teaching Special Education Students

Section D:

Collaboration/Consultation

Section E:

The IEP

Section F:

Physical Handicaps

At one time or another
everyone has special needs.

Students receiving Special Education services will comprise a part of virtually all regular education classrooms. A number of questions and concerns are often expressed by beginning teachers preparing to work with students who receive Special Education services. This section addresses some common questions and issues in the education of students with special needs.

The term Special Education conjures up many thoughts and images in the minds of teachers and students. Consider the following definitions of a Special Education teacher:

- Special Education teachers teach students with special needs.

- Special Education teachers use special techniques to meet the needs of students.

The first definition focuses on the student as the critical component in determining who is a Special Education teacher. The second definition centers on the approach, rather than the student, in determining what constitutes Special Education. Viewing instruction from the second perspective, any teacher employing special techniques to address student needs is a Special Educator. This instruction-centered view forms the basis for our philosophy toward Special Education.

Will Special Education students be placed in my classroom?

Yes. Regardless of the area in which you plan to teach, students who receive Special Education services will likely be placed in your classroom. The guidelines for determining the best instructional placements for students with special needs were established by Public Law 94-142. Several components of P.L. 94-142 detail who receives Special Education services and where these students will receive services.

Section A

Least Restrictive Environment

What is the Least Restrictive Environment?

The least restrictive environment (LRE) is the setting that best meets the needs of the student. The term is often interpreted as a mandate that students with disabilities be mainstreamed in regular classrooms. For some students, regular classroom placement is often the environment where the most learning can take place. For other students, however, resource room programs are determined to be the LRE, and for certain students, self-contained special educational classrooms may be required. Determination of the LRE is a primary component of all placement decisions. The determination is not made by one individual and the decision is not based on any one specific criterion. A multi-disciplinary team, often comprised of a special education teacher, the student's regular classroom teacher, school psychologist, parents, and other professionals associated with the student makes decisions regarding the program that will best meet an individual student's needs. In determining the LRE, the following points should be addressed:

Which placement will result in the most growth for the student both academically and socially?

Two important points to consider when evaluating placements are:

- Can the designated placement meet the student's needs?

- Does the placement provide interaction with non-disabled students while ensuring academic success?

By definition, the LRE is the placement in which the student most benefits from instruction. The requirement that a student be placed in the least restrictive environment ensures that the students' needs are met in the best possible way. Often, the LRE is determined to be a regular education classroom setting, perhaps with resource room support. The rationale behind this decision is based on research demonstrating that the most effective way to teach student behaviors that they are lacking is to expose them to others who demonstrate the behaviors. In the case of pro-social skills; for example, it seems to follow that a student lacking age-appropriate interpersonal skills is more likely to benefit from exposure to students who lack the appropriate skills. This seemingly logical approach does not, however, ensure that the student will learn appropriate skills merely by being exposed to them. Direct instruction on target skills is required to ensure that students master them.

Instruction on specific skills is often provided via resource room pullout programs, and at times through consultation and collaboration between the regular classroom teacher and the special education teacher, the school psychologist, or other behavioral or instructional experts. To most effectively address the student's needs in the regular classroom, as well as ensure that the other students in the classroom benefit from instruction, the teacher should:

- Keep an organized classroom learning environment.

- Provide an abundance of success for all students.

- Hold high expectations.

- Devise a structured behavior management program.

- Maintain close working relationships with the special education teacher and other staff members.

- Collect data so that the effects of instruction-based decisions can be evaluated and modified.

- Focus on teaching self-management and self-monitoring natural cues and adjusts his or her own behavior.

P.L. 94-142 calls for placement of students in the Least Restrictive Environment (LRE). Students are to be educated in settings which are most "normal" and in which the student will receive the most benefit from instruction. LRE does not dictate that all students will benefit the most from placement in the regular classroom setting, however it does call for placement—to the maximum degree possible—in the regular education setting.

Placement of students with special needs is best viewed as a continuum from most normal placement (the regular classroom) to most restrictive placement (a private in-patient institution). The Cascade Model of Special Education Service illustrates the continuum on which multi-disciplinary teams may determine the most appropriate (least restrictive) placement for individual students. (See figure on following page.)

> *Super Suggestion:*
> *For some students, the Least Restrictive Environment may be the regular education classroom, for others, resource room assistance for specific subject areas may be recommended. Other students may receive instruction in a self-contained classroom, whereas others may receive instruction in special schools for students with disabilities.*

Cascade Model of Special Education Service

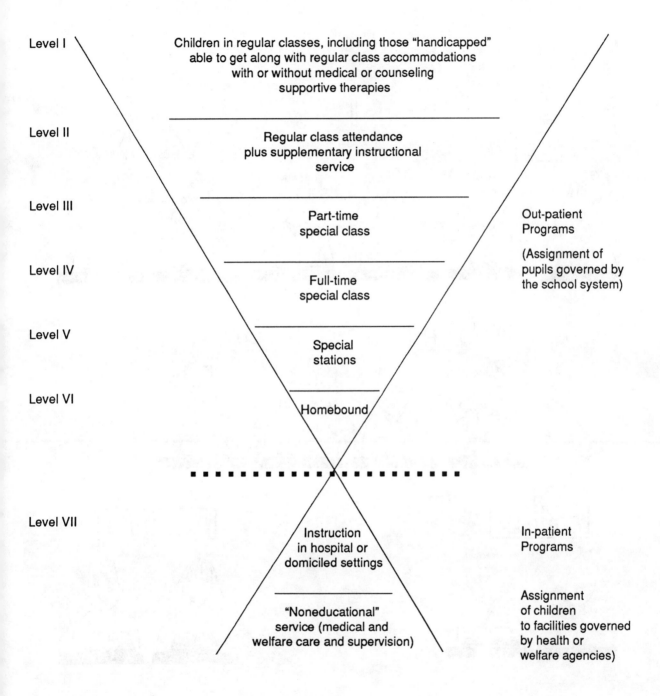

Level I — Children in regular classes, including those "handicapped" able to get along with regular class accommodations with or without medical or counseling supportive therapies

Level II — Regular class attendance plus supplementary instructional service

Level III — Part-time special class — Out-patient Programs (Assignment of pupils governed by the school system)

Level IV — Full-time special class

Level V — Special stations

Level VI — Homebound

Level VII — Instruction in hospital or domiciled settings — In-patient Programs

"Noneducational" service (medical and welfare care and supervision) — Assignment of children to facilities governed by health or welfare agencies)

From E. Deno, "Special Education as Developmental Capital," *Exceptional Children* 1970, 37, 229-237.

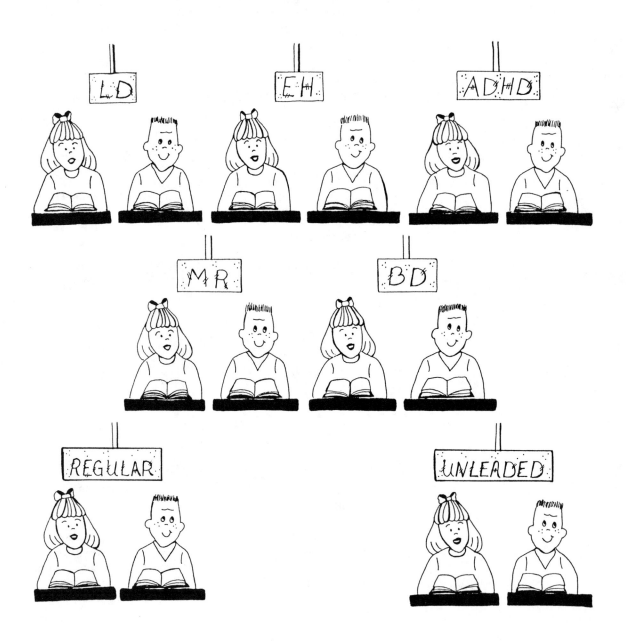

Section B

Categorical Labels

What "types" of Special Education students will I encounter?

First, let's take a look at the way that question is phrased. As educators, we are not concerned with "types" of special education students. In fact, we have little need to refer to students as "types" at all. There is presently a strong trend in the educational community to employ what is referred to as the *person first* approach when describing students who receive Special Education services. The *person first* approach reflects the philosophy that regardless of disability, all students are people first and foremost. We should therefore refer to them as students WITH a disability, rather than DISABLED students.

Effective instruction is instruction which best meets each student's needs at a given point in time. From this perspective, the type of disability has little instructional relevance. Our primary charge as educators is to determine the most effective way to teach each student—regardless of categorical label.

Categorical labels include learning disabilities, emotional/behavioral disorders, speech or language impaired, mental retardation, hearing impaired or deaf, multi-handicapped, orthopedically impaired, other health impaired, visually handicapped, and deaf-blind. In addition, students may receive special services based on other factors—such as socioeconomic status. Students experiencing reading difficulties who are from low SES areas may qualify for Chapter One funding. Other students experiencing academic difficulty may simply be labeled "at-risk". The difference between a student labeled "at-risk" and a student officially labeled, for example, "learning disabled," may be very difficult to identify. The instructional utility of categorical labels is extremely limited.

If categorical labels don't help decide what or how to teach, why do we use them?

Categorical labels do serve several purposes. Ultimately they indicate what type of services a student qualify for—which enables the student (via the school) to receive federal funding to support his or her special instruction. In addition to funding concerns, categorical labels provide educators and researchers with a general way to describe groups of students demonstrating similar areas of difficulty. If a teacher is interested in reading about techniques which are effective in addressing behavior of students with severe behavioral problems, he or she may look at the literature on students with behavioral disorders. Categorical labels are also used in teacher training and certification.

Today, we do not place a great deal of emphasis on educators diagnosing disabilities. In fact, it is not clear that diagnosis is an appropriate part of the classroom teacher's responsibilities. As educators, we must focus on ALTERABLE VARIABLES—those variables that a teacher can directly identify and remediate—things that you can do something about. Let us consider two approaches to determining what to teach. A teacher could spend a great deal of time diagnosing the underlying cause of the student's disability—for example, it may be inferred that the student has discalculia—an inability to do mathematics problems. There is no doubt that tests claiming to identify students with discalculia are commercially available. *So what happens after this disability is diagnosed?* If effective instruction is to follow, the teacher would then identify missing sub-skills and strategies and remediate them directly. Now consider another approach—what would have happened if the classroom teacher choose not to spend time with diagnosis, but instead began by identifying which sub-skills and strategies the student was missing—and then proceeded to teach those areas directly? That student would be on their way to remediating the problem.

Is the students' "disability" the cause of their behavior?

Even though the "source" of the student's problem may very well be an internal disorder—a learning disability, mental retardation, a behavioral disorder—this information is of limited educational relevance. Special educators in the past were highly concerned with identifying the "type" of disorder that the student demonstrated—was the student's problem due to a processing deficit? dyslexia? a learning disability? A great deal of time may be devoted to determining the precise label for the source of a student's problem—however, the educational approach will be the same—identify the exact skills and strategies that the student lacks and teach them directly. Research has shown that the most effective way to remediate academic and pro-social deficits is through direct instruction of the target skill.

Principal's Principles: For example, rather than referring to a "mentally retarded student", we would describe this person as a student with mental retardation. A "learning dis-abled student" would be referred to as a student with a learning disability.

Principal's Principles: Focusing only on ALTERABLE VARIABLES will guide effective instructional experiences for students receiving special services.

Principal's Principles: It is impossible to determine, given the descriptor "at-risk" versus the label "learning disabled" which student will require more instruction.

Section C

Questions about Teaching Special Education Students

Does medication help students?

Treatment of behavioral and academic learning problems with medication remains a controversial issue. Ultimately, it is important to realize that medication that may have a positive effect on student behavior does not teach the student new or appropriate pro-social skills. Regardless of whether the student is receiving medication, he or she will likely require direct instruction of the skill. Medications have been researched the most with children with behavioral problems. Research has shown that in some cases, medication can produce positive effects on a student's attention. However, opponents raise questions regarding undesirable effects the medication can have on the student's perception of control. The student may come to attribute more power to the medication than to his or her own ability to control or monitor personal behavior. The development of self-management or self-monitoring skills may be impaired by the student's belief that he or she is not able to control personal behavior.

Of particular concern is the way that need for medication is determined. Instances in which teachers have recommended that parents seek medication for their children are not uncommon. This type of recommendation is clearly outside the role of the classroom teacher. From a teaching perspective, the best approach is to be aware of students who are receiving medication. Administration times, dosage problems, and inconsistencies in administration can have dramatic effects on student behavior. Teachers should note these types of problems and report to the school medical staff and the student's parents immediately. Side effects of medication may include falling asleep, becoming excessively thirsty or hungry, demonstrating tremors, or developing blank stares.

There is not a special set of approaches for working with students who are receiving medication. A focus on identifying specific skills, evaluating student performance, and directly addressing skill deficits will ensure that these students benefit from instruction.

What should my expectations be for students who receive special education services?

Ultimately, your expectations should be the same as for students who do not receive special services. When we conduct evaluation we take a student's behavior and compare it to a standard. The degree to which the student's behavior deviates from that standard determines the significance of the problem. One of the most detrimental views adopted by teachers of students with special needs may be referred to as the "you can't expect as much" position.

Frequently, teachers will view students who receive special services as not ABLE to perform at the levels expected of other students in the classroom. If, for example, the criteria for acceptable performance on multiplication facts is 100% for the "regular" students (or students who have not been officially "labeled"), the teacher may lower the criteria to 80% for students receiving special education services—because you can't expect as much from them. So what would be the outcome of this lowered criteria? Aside from serious impact on the student's view of him or her self, one outcome is quite predictable—the student with the special education label is not likely to ever reach a functionally appropriate level of expertise at that skill.

For example, goals for students receiving special education services are commonly set at 80%. Where did the 80% criteria come from? Good question. Numerous authors have investigated the literature in search of an answer. It is hypothesized that since 80% is viewed as "C" or "Average" work, this level is assumed to be appropriate for special education students. What does lowering the criteria result in? For example, lets consider a real-life skill; pumping gasoline. If the criteria for "regular" education students is 100% accuracy, a teacher holding the "you can't expect as much" position may reduce the goal for a special education student to 80% accuracy. This lowered criteria would result in 8 out of 10 cars receiving the correct type of gas, and 2 out of 10 receiving something else. The 80% criteria is not often functional outside of the classroom.

Teacher expectations represent goals for which a teacher holds students accountable. These goals or expectations serve as a standard by which the teacher assesses the students' current perfor-

> **Principal's Principles:** Whenever we choose to lower our criteria for acceptable performance, we ensure that the student will not be provided with the opportunity to successfully master that skill.

mance or functioning. Teachers hold both academic and social behavioral expectations for their students. For students in the regular classrooms, teacher expectations center on the behaviors necessary for successful participation in adult life.

If all students are held to the same criteria, won't students who receive Special Education become frustrated?

Teaching any student at a level for which they are not prepared will likely result in frustration. Recall that an appropriate level of instruction is one in which the student has the necessary sub-skills and strategies. This is the level at which instruction for special education students—and all students should be delivered. The amount of time that it takes a student receiving special services to attain the ultimate goal may be extended, instruction on sub-skills and strategies may be more focused, but the ultimate criteria for acceptable performance is not lowered. If 100% accuracy is necessary to ensure, for example, that a student can make change as a cashier, then 100% accuracy is the criteria for acceptable performance for all students—including those who receive special education services.

> **Principal's Principles:** *Expectations for students receiving special education services should ultimately be the same as for those established for their "non-disabled" peers.*

Expectations which are "too high" will frustrate anyone—whether they are receiving special services or not. Remember that teaching the appropriate objective means teaching the objective that the student is ready to learn. Ready to learn, for our purposes means, teaching the objective which the student possesses the necessary sub-skills and strategies to learn. The term "ready to learn" does not mean that the student is permitted to select his or her own curricula or educational focus. This approach will ensure that all students are provided with the opportunity to master the skills necessary for functioning outside of the classroom.

Should Special Education students be grouped with other low-functioning students?

The effective education literature has shown that heterogeneous grouping is an effective instructional approach. Combining students of different performance levels results in overall growth of all students involved. This approach holds true for students who receive special education services. For example, if a student is receiving special education services for a reading problem, they are likely to benefit from exposure to reading instruction in the regular classroom, as well as instruction in the resource room setting.

Students receiving special education services for behavioral problems often demonstrate immature behavior. There is often disagreement as to the best approach for educating these students.

How can a regular classroom teacher address the needs of students with learning problems?

Designing instruction for students who receive special education services may seem overwhelming in the regular classroom. It may appear that a student does not have any of the skills expected of the other students in the classroom. How can the regular education teacher provide instruction on every skill that the special education student is missing—while at the same time advancing the other students through the curriculum? One key to effective programming for special education students is to carefully pinpoint missing sub-skills and strategies and provide direct instruction on those skills.

Many students who receive special education services do not readily demonstrate any of the skills expected in the regular classroom—it may be assumed that they need to be taught everything. The efficiency of setting out to teach a student every skill is questionable. An alternative approach is to first consider the desired behavior—the student either displays it (DOES) or not (DOESN'T). If the student DOES, we aren't too concerned. If the student doesn't, we must go a step beyond and determine if it is a CAN or CAN'T behavior.

- ■ CAN behaviors are those in which the student possesses necessary sub-skills and strategies to perform as is expected. As we will see in a moment, just because a student CAN doesn't mean that they will perform the skill or behavior.

- ■ CAN'T refers to behaviors in which the student lacks necessary sub-skills to perform the task. These students have never demonstrated the desired behavior, and because they lack prerequisite skills, are not at the moment able to demonstrate the behavior.

If we can determine that the student does possess the prerequisite skills (CAN), then our instructional focus would be on strategies for combining those skills to perform the task. The student may be able to perform the skill, but does not attend to environmental cues, does not determine which skill is called for in specific situations.

> *Coach's Corner:*
> *When considering the most effective placement for students with behavioral problems, consider the following question—would students who act immature be more likely to benefit from models who also demonstrate immature behavior—or from peers who demonstrate socially appropriate behavior?*

If we determine that the student lacks necessary prerequisite skills (**CAN'T**), those skills must be directly taught. Distinguishing between the need to teach sub-skills and strategies will make instructional attempts more efficient. Considering performance deficits from this perspective will help ensure that learning is viewed as an interaction—between the teacher, the student, and the curriculum—rather than focusing solely on the student as the source of the problem.

What if this seems to conflict with my instructional philosophy or with the philosophies of other teachers?

Many classroom teachers have differing philosophies. Some may be very structured and skill-based, while others may take a more holistic view of education. Both teachers may be effective in accomplishing the ultimate goal—enhancing the student's education. Trying things which deviate from overall philosophies may often be in order when working with students who are behind in the curriculum. For example, if a discovery approach doesn't appear to be working with an individual student, perhaps a skill-based approach, coupled with opportunity to engage in cooperative learning activities may be effective.

Special educators often focus on individualization of instruction, which refers to the efforts made to ensure that each student is receiving instruction that meets his or her needs. This does not mean that these students are held to a lesser expectation of performance. However, short-term expectations may have to be adjusted to account for the student's current level of performance and the path to the goal may have to be broken into more specific steps. The expected date of mastery or amount of time necessary to accomplish a given skill may require an increase for some students. Evaluation of student progress, as well as evaluation of the effectiveness of interventions, centers on the students making progress that will permit attainment of both short- and long-term goals. Long- term goals are the curriculum objectives that are in place for all students. The curriculum is not changed for students receiving special education services. It represents skills that the society, the community, the teachers, parents, and students hold as important, then all students should have the opportunity to move toward these objectives. However, the process by which they meet goals or expectations may vary among students.

Principal's Principles:
The critical point is that the expectations or ultimate goals are not altered for students with special needs.

The following points are important to keep in mind when setting expectations for all students:

- Use data-based decision-rules to guide instructional decisions.

- Do not change or lower curriculum expectations for students in special education. They also need the opportunity to receive instruction geared toward optimizing their progress toward those goals.

- Assess the student's competence at prerequisite sub-skills and strategies for combining those sub-skills to perform tasks.

- Use continuous monitoring of performance to assess the student's progress toward the goal.

- Adjust teaching accordingly when the student strays from the projected path toward the goal.

- Employ direct instruction of the necessary sub-skills and strategies.

- Realize that accuracy is only one way that a student may demonstrate proficiency at a task. Focus on teaching higher-level thinking skills (strategies for combining sub-skills to perform other tasks or strategies for recognizing environmental cues and monitoring the appropriateness of ones own pro-social behavior) to bring the student to mastery and automaticity levels.

Section D

Collaboration/Consultation

Differing philosophies toward instruction of students with disabilities will be clearly evident in classroom settings. Often, students emerge from their teacher training program with ideals and philosophies which appear to differ dramatically from those of their cooperating teachers, or from other teachers in the school. Working with students who receive special education services will require cooperation and collaboration with a great number of professionals in the school. The special education student's program will be designed by members of a multi- disciplinary team (MDT), often consisting of the classroom teacher, special education teacher, school psychologist, parents, speech and hearing personnel, as will as other auxiliary service personnel.

As with other aspects of education, teachers who hold diametrically opposing views may both be exceedingly effective in education the student. As a beginning teacher, now is a good time to develop your collaboration skills. It is helpful to keep in mind that you will be working with teachers who received their training at different institutions, over different time periods, when different philosophies and practices were stressed.

What types of assessment and evaluation will I need to conduct with students receiving special education services?

Assessment and evaluation are conducted to determine the most effective approaches to instructional interventions for specific students. Assessment refers to collecting information through observation, administering tests, or recording student responses. Functional assessment refers to approaches of measuring student performance which yield specific information for remediation of problems. Evaluation is a process of comparing a student's behavior to a standard and noting the discrepancy (Howell & Morehead, 1987). The standard represents the "desired" behavior—what the teacher feels that the student should be doing. The evaluator's standard may be influenced by factors such as the behavior of other students, societal beliefs, classroom norms, and categorical definitions.

Coach's Corner: Effective communication within this setting will have a dramatic impact on the effectiveness of the student's educational program.

Principal's Principles: Working with multi- disciplinary teams requires diplomacy.

Student behavior can be evaluated with respect to various performance standards and through a variety of observation approaches. Ideally, a functional analysis of student behavior using multi-method approaches to assessment should be adopted. This approach to evaluating student behavior may incorporate ratings and views of student behavior or academic performance from the perspectives of several people involved with the student: the student's teacher, other teachers in the school, the student's parents, peers; and the student himself or herself may serve an evaluator of the target behavior.

A data-based approach should be employed when evaluating students. Direct observations and recordings of the students' ongoing performance will assist in making instructional decisions. The following points should be considered when devising an evaluation approach:

■ There should be a clear purpose for testing.

■ If items or questions are presented, each item should be keyed to an objective.

■ Objectives should be defined operationally and should clearly state the four necessary components: learner, condition, behavior, and criteria.

■ The measure should assess the strategies needed to perform the objective successfully.

■ The measure should provide an adequate sample of student behavior.

■ The measure should be presented in an appropriate format.

■ The measure should be easy to use and interpret.

> **Coach's Corner:**
> *Two types of decisions can be made from assessment information—classification decisions and treatment decisions.*
> ***Classification decisions*** *include the assignment of categorical labels such as behaviorally disordered, mentally retarded, learning disabled, placement in special programs, assignment to grade levels, and so forth.*
> ***Treatment decisions*** *include "what-to-teach" and "how to teach" decisions. The decisions addressed in this section focus primarily on assessment and evaluation for the purpose of making treatment decisions—the types of decisions made by teachers.*

Section E

THE IEP

Will the IEP help me work with the student? The answer ultimately depends on the quality of the Individualized Education Program (IEP). The IEP should provide specific instructional objectives for the student. These objectives should be operationally defined and directly observable. The criteria for acceptable performance should be stated in a measurable, countable form. The method of assuring the student's progress toward this goal should be clearly stated. In essence, the IEP provides a plan for both remediating and evaluation the effects of the intervention on student performance. It guides a teach-test-teach approach of intervention. Formulation of instructional decisions is based on a continuous monitoring of the student's progress toward the goals stated in the IEP.

The IEP also serves as a means of communicating the goals to the student's parents and teachers, the school psychologist, and others.

Information about a student's previous performance should not limit expectations for the student in the new placement setting. The amount of energy required to obtain the information should be proportional to its value in making instructional decisions. Talking to past teachers, discussing concerns with the student's parents and school psychologists can provide valuable information. However, these sources might also provide a distorted picture of what is actually taking place. Therefore, it is important to take into consideration interventions that have been tried in the past, as well as situations in which the student performed successfully or demonstrated appropriate behavior.

Coach's Corner: In and of itself, the IEP does not ensure successful application of a special education program, but it does provide a means of communicating objectives and specifying intervention and evaluation procedures regarding the student. Each of these pieces of information provides important information about the student.

P.L. 94-142 requires that an Individualized Education Program be developed and implemented for each student receiving special education services. Each IEP must contain the following components:

- A documentation of the student's current level of educational performance.

- Annual goals or the attainments expected by the end of the school year.

- Short-term objectives, stated in instructional terms, which are the intermediate steps leading to mastery of annual goals.

- Documentation of the particular special education that will be provided to the student.

- Documentation of the particular related services, if any, that will be provided to the student.

- An indication of the extent of time a student will participate in the regular education program.

- Projected dates for initiating services and the anticipated duration of services.

- Appropriate objective criteria, evaluation procedures, and schedules for determining mastery of short-term objectives, at least on an annual basis.

- A statement explaining that the student's placement is indeed in the Least Restrictive Environment.

Accountability

All services included on the document must be provided and the goals and objectives must be addressed as stated. The school must also ensure that the IEP is revised and that it continues to represent appropriate programming for the student.

Should the focus of the special education student's program be Academic or Social Behavior?

As with all students, an effective behavior management system and effective teaching strategies will ensure that the student excels in academic and social behavioral areas. Enabling a student to be academically successful often leads to fewer behavioral problems in the classroom. Likewise, an effective behavior

Super Suggestion: Curricular choices should be made based on the student's needs, and they will be most beneficial and motivational if used in conjunction with effective teaching strategies and effective behavior management systems.

management system will lead to fewer behavior problems, thereby enabling the student to perform better academically.

Which instructional techniques are most appropriate?

Effective teaching practices will maximize the likelihood of student success. Effective teaching strategies are techniques that have been found to significantly increase student learning and decrease related behavioral problems. The following characteristics of effective classrooms are arranged in two groups: 1) strategies for individual lessons and 2) strategies to use throughout the school day:

Individual Lessons

- Clearly communicate to students the goal/purpose of the lesson.

- Present a well-organized, sequenced lesson.

- Use a lead-test-model strategy when presenting new material. Explain key concepts of the lesson (lead), demonstrate how to perform the skill of the lesson (model) through examples and non-examples of the skill, and finally, require the student to independently perform the skill (test).

- Give clear instructional feedback (explain why an answer/response is correct or incorrect).

- Begin each lesson with the expectation that students can and will learn the new skill.

- Ensure student success in each lesson by programming to promote high rates of student accuracy.

- Use quick pacing during instruction.

Throughout the Day

- Prompt and provide smooth transitions between lessons and activities.

- Distribute opportunities to practice new skills.

- Use natural contingencies for student success (grades, verbal praise, privileges).

- Provide and focus on positive interactions with students.

INDIVIDUAL EDUCATION PROGRAM

Date 3-1-92

(1) Student

Name: Joe S.
School: Adams
Grade: 5
Current Placement: Regular Class/Resource Room

Date of Birth: 10-1-80   Age: 11-5

(2) Committee

Mrs. Wrens Principal Initial
Mrs. Snow Regular Teacher
Mr. LaJoie Counselor
Mr. Thomas Resource Teacher
Mr. Ryan School Psychologist
Mrs. S. Parent
Joe S. Student

EP from 3-15-91 to 3-15-92

(3) Present Level of Educational Functioning	(4) Annual Goal Statements	(5) Instructional Objectives	(6) Objective Criteria and Evaluation
MATH Strengths 1. Can successfully compute addition and subtraction problems to two places with regrouping and zeros. 2. Knows 100 basic multiplication facts. Weaknesses 1. Frequently makes computational errors on problems with which he has had experience. 2. Does not complete seatwork. Key Math total score of 2.1 Grade Equivalent.	Joe will apply knowledge of regrouping in addition and renaming in subtraction to four-digit numbers.	1. When presented with 20 additional problems of 3-digit numbers requiring two renamings the student will compute the answer at a rate of one problem per minute and an accuracy of 90%. 2. When presented with 20 subtraction problems of 3-digit numbers requiring two renamings the student will compute the answer at a rate of one problem per minute with 90% accuracy. 3. When presented with 20 addition problems of 4-digit numbers requiring three renamings the student will compute the answer at a rate of one problem per minute and an accuracy of 90%. 4. When present with 20 subtraction problems of 4-digit numbers requiring three renamings the student will compute the answer at a rate of one problem per minute with 90% accuracy.	Teacher made tests (weekly) Teacher made tests (weekly) Teacher made tests (weekly)

185

Section F

Physical Handicaps

The term Special Education often conjures up an image of a certain type of student. The typical view of the Special Education student is one in which we can see the handicap—the idea that special education students physically appear different. As previously noted, this is not the case with the majority of students receiving special education services. Students with physical handicaps represent approximately 2% of the students receiving public education. This constitutes about 4% of the students who receive special education services. In addition to learning problems, students may require special services related to their specific physical handicaps. Students with physical handicaps may have difficulties due to neurological, orthopedic, or chronic health disorders. Although the category or "type" of physical disability indicates very little about the actual needs of the students, the terms do provide a general structure for referral, identification, and intervention.

As an educator, your role is to accommodate these student so that they have maximum opportunity to benefit from instruction in the classroom. In meeting a student who has a physical handicap, the tendency is typically to focus on the handicap itself—attempting to better understand the nature and cause of the physical problem. It is critically important to keep in mind that, although awareness of characteristics of physical disabilities will enable the classroom teacher to make decisions and modifications that will facilitate student learning, knowing the type and cause of the disability does not provide all of the information necessary to deliver effective instruction.

This section outlines considerations for students with physical disabilities. The areas of focus have been divided into the following categories: Orthopedic Impairments; Hearing Impairments; Visual Impairments; and Other Health Impairments

The recommendations represent good practice—they are designed to effectively guide your investigation of any impairment that you may encounter.

Orthopedic Impairments

Orthopedically impaired children and other health impaired children comprise approximately 2% of all children receiving special education services. Orthopedic impairments include Cerebral Palsy, Muscular Dystrophy, Spina Bifida, Juvenile Rheumatoid Arthritis, and students who have had amputations. Academic and social performance of students with orthopedic impairments may vary greatly depending on the age of onset, level of severity, and the extend of physical involvement. Some orthopedic handicaps also involve what are referred to as secondary impairments. These often include speech problems, vision and hearing problems, or mental retardation. Orthopedic impairments typically restrict mobility and often employ adaptive equipment to facilitate productivity. Students with limited mobility may need assistance with a range of activities—from daily maneuvering within the classroom and around the school building to participating in physical activities and learning to write or use a keyboard. Performance of students with orthopedic impairments may be enhanced through the following adaptations:

- Eliminate or adapt architectural barriers. Increase accessibility through the use of ramps, broad aisles.

- Adjust desks, toilet facilities and drinking fountains.

- Adjust curriculum requirements by providing alternative means of completing the assignment. Investigate use of computers and other assistive devices.

Students with orthopedic impairments are often quite aware of teacher attitudes towards their differences. The extra efforts and accommodations required by others may appear to the student as a burden to the classroom teacher and peers. It is important for the educator to relate clear information to the student regarding attitudes and views toward adaptation.

Coach's Corner:
Educators should understand the operation and limitations of the specific equipment used by the student. Students may use wheelchairs, braces or crutches to enhance their mobility. Teachers should consult with the physical therapist, parents, and the STUDENT regarding operation and maintenance of specific equipment.

Principal's Principles:
An open and accepting environment creates the most opportunities for achievement of all students.

187

Hearing Impairments

Hearing impairments effect three out of approximately one-hundred school children. The literature identifies two levels of hearing impairment—deaf and hard of hearing—each based on the severity of the hearing loss. As defined by PL 94-142, the term "deaf" means that the hearing impairment is so severe that with or without amplification, the child's educational performance is adversely affected. The term "hard of hearing" can be understood as any impairment that affects a child's academic performance, but is not included under the definition of "deaf." Because of the ambiguity of these definitions, it is best to understand hearing impairments as related to three factors:

1. Nature of hearing impairment

2. Degree of hearing impairment

3. Age at which impairment occurred.

Knowledge of each of these areas will provide the educator with a better under standing of the needs of individual students with hearing problems.

Secondary impairments that may occur with hearing impairment include problems with perception, speech, communication, and social interaction. Through appropriate interventions, each of these secondary problems can be effectively addressed. Social and behavioral problems associated with hearing impairment are often overlooked by educators. Depending on severity of the impairment, students with hearing loss may exhibit seemingly inappropriate social interactions. Often these students may not be able to appropriately monitor the social environment for necessary cues, and may exhibit frustration from lack of effective communication. Educators should be aware of behavioral aspects which may be associated with hearing impairment.

Screening

Screening for hearing problems has become a routine feature in the schools. Although formal assessment is conducted in public schools, the classroom teacher is in a position to recognize possible problems early on. Educators should be aware of common indicators of hearing impairments. Observation of the following types of behavior may signal the need for closer investigation:

- Student turns one side of the head toward the speaker or touches the ears while trying to listen.

■ The student demonstrates delayed language development (compared to same-age peers or proficiency criteria).

■ The student is constantly asking for comments made by the teacher and peers to be repeated.

■ The student exhibits inappropriate responses to questions. The student's responses seem out-of-place given the context and content of the question.

■ The student often complains of ear aches, constant colds or sore throats.

Visual Impairments

Some form of visual impairment is experienced by approximately 20 percent of the population. Like other physical impairments, the degree of disability is related to the severity of the impairment. From an educational perspective, visual handicaps may be referred to as one of three "types:"

1. Blindness—vision is worse than 20/200.

2. Partial sight—students are unable to perform ordinary tasks with correction.

3. Visual defects—easily correctable; astigmatism, nearsightedness.

Identification and Screening

Educators should familiarize themselves with indicators of possible vision problems. These include:

- squinting and rubbing eyes
- frequently blinking
- inflamed or watery eyes
- dizziness or headaches

Adaptations for visual impairments may include seating the student close to the board, providing more detailed verbal explanations of written assignments, ensuring appropriate lighting near the student's work area, or employing adaptive or augmentative equipment such as braille, enlarged print, or electronic reading and writing devices. As with the previously discussed disabilities, teachers should monitor students use of equipment and assist students with participating in the classroom activities to the greatest extent possible.

Health Impairments

This category of handicaps refers to those conditions that involve severe communication, educational and developmental problems which adversely affect the student's education performance. Educators should be aware of these health problems and understand the effects of these problems on their particular student's academic performance. Some of the more severe problems that a teacher may encounter include: Seizure Disorders (Epilepsy); Cystic Fibrosis; Tuberculosis; Rheumatic Fever; Juvenile Diabetes; Sickle Cell Anemia; Congenital Heart Disease; Asthma; and Severe Allergies.

Health impairments may vary greatly in terms of severity and prognosis. A primary responsibility of school personnel serving students with health impairments is that of collaboration with the teacher and medical professionals. Students may require a range of services—from routine medical care to frequent, intensive medical aid. Some school districts have specific procedural guidelines covering the educator's role regarding medical care and support services, while others may have no written guidelines at all. It is the responsibility of the teacher to remain aware of a child's needs for medical care, and to familiarize themselves with district and school policy.

Students who are chronically ill tend to have higher rates of absenteeism which in itself often has a dramatic effect on academic performance. Considerations when addressing the needs of students with health impairments include:

- Schedule to insure maximum time on-task.

- Be aware of possible side effects of medications and what to do should you observe possible effects.

- Be aware of the limitations of specific health impairments. For example, students with diabetes may need to eat measured amounts of food at prescribed intervals and take medication regularly. An asthmatic child may be required to avoid participation in extended physical activities. Educators should gather information on any limitations—through dialogue with school medical personnel, parents, and the STUDENT.

As with all disabilities, students with health impairments are ensured the opportunity to develop academically and participate in educational programs to the greatest extent possible. The educator plays a key role in maintaining effective services for students with physical impairments. The current trend in Special Education is that of cross categorical instruction—with as little as possible focus on labeling. Obvious physical handicaps can be effectively addressed through analysis of each task as it relates to the particular child's disability. It is essential that although modifications and adaptations may be necessary to ensure effective experiences for students with physical handicaps, care must be taken to provide all students with access to mastery of the curriculum.

Related Readings

The following resources may provide more specific information on areas related to special and remedial education—and overall effective instruction.

Journals

Exceptionality. Research and issues in the education of students with special needs. Published by the Council for Exceptional Children.

Remedial and Special Education. Deals with practice related issues in special and remedial education. Focus ranges from specific instructional techniques, to issues in integration and mainstreaming. Published by Pro-Ed.

Teaching Exceptional Children. A practitioner-based journal focusing primarily on classroom-based and community-based interventions. Published by the Council for Exceptional Children.

Education and Treatment in Mental Retardation. Focuses on research-based information related to students with mental retardation. Published by the Division for Mental Retardation, Council for Exceptional Children.

Behavioral Disorders. A research based journal published by the Council for children with behavioral disorders division of the Council for Exceptional Children. Research-based articles addressing issues in the treatment and remediation of behavioral problems. Focus addresses both practitioner applications, and definition and policy issues The council for Children with Behavioral Disorders issues position papers addressing specific issues on behavioral disorders through this journal.

Journal of Learning Disabilities. Published 10 times a year by Pro-Ed. Addresses research-based and theoretical/policy issues in the education of students with learning disabilities.

Learning Disabilities Research: Learning Disabilities Focus. The division for Learning Disabilities publishes each of these, twice a year.

Learning Disability Quarterly. Focuses on classroom-based applications of research on learning disabilities. Published four times a year by the Council for Learning Disabilities.

Journal of Speech and Hearing Disorders. Published by the

American Speech-Language-Hearing Association (ASHA). Addresses issues in communication disorders.

Gifted Child Quarterly. Published by the National ASsociation for Gifted Children.

Journal of Early Intervention. Published by the Division for Early Childhood, Councils for Exceptional Children.

Topics in Early Childhood Special Education. Pro-Ed.

American Annals of the Deaf. Addresses issues in education of students who are deaf and hearing impaired. Published by the Conference of Educational Administrators Serving the Deaf.

Journal of Visual Impairment and Blindness. Published by the American Foundation of the Blind. Addresses issues across educational and social areas related to visual impairment.

Journal of The Association for Persons with Severe Handicaps (JASH). Addresses assessment and intervention across severe handicapping conditions. Published by the Association for Persons with Severe Handicaps.

Books

Cainine, D., Silbert, J., & Kameenui, E.J. (1990). *Direct instruction reading* (2nd ed.). Columbus, OH: Merrill.

Heward, W.L., & Orlansky, M.D. (1992). *Exceptional children: An introductory survey of special education* (fourth ed). New York: Macmillan.

Howell, K.W., & Morehead, M.K. (1978). *Curriculum-based Assessment in Special and Remedial Education.* Columbus, OH: Merrill.

Kameenui E.J., & Simmons, D.C. (1990). *Designing instruction strategies.* Columbus, OH: Merrill

Kauffman, J.M. (1989). *Characteristics of behavior disorders of children and youth* (fourth ed.). Columbus, OH: Merrill.

Kerr, M.N., & Nelson, C.M. (1989). *Strategies for managing behavior problems in the classroom* (2nd ed.). Columbus, OH: Merrill.

Lovitt, T.C. (1989). *Introduction to Learning Disabilities.* Boston: Allyn & Bacon.

Sailor, W., Anderson, J.L., Halvorsen, A.T., Doering, K., filler,

J., & Goetz, L. (1989). *The comprehensive local school: Regular education for all students with disabilities.* Baltimore, MD: Brookes.

Silbert, J., Cainine, D., & Stein, M. (1981). *Direct instruction mathematics.* Columbus, OH: Merrill.

Organizations

Council for Exceptional Children. This is the primary organization for professionals in Special Education. CEC encompasses numerous divisions, each addressing a specific area of exceptionality. 1920 Association Drive, Reston, VA 22091.

Cystic Fibrosis Foundation, 6000 Executive Boulevard, Rockville, MD 20852

Epilepsy Foundation of America, 45331 Garden City Drive, Landover, MD 20785.

Juvenile Diabetes Association, 23 East 26th Street, New York NY 10010.

Muscular Dystrophy Association, 810 Seventh Avenue, New York, NY 10019.

Chapter 10

Tips from a Veteran First Year Teacher
(What I Didn't Learn Until I Taught)

Teachers who have survived the first year of teaching offer the clearest perspective of classroom realities. Talking to both novices and veterans will help you persevere during the first year of teaching.

1. It takes time to make a difference in the political aspects of the school and community. Focus on making a difference with students before you assume the role of "revamping" the system.

2. It takes special skill to work effectively with a paraprofessional. Instructional assistants are frequently from the community and may have been serving in their positions for several years. Establish time at the outset of the school year to communicate about the necessity for scheduling routine planning sessions. Think about and talk about collaboration and team building with instructional assistants who may be assigned to you.

3. Take extraordinary care of your physical health, i.e. diet, exercise, regular sleep.

4. Establish and maintain a support system. Include your family, your new colleagues, friends, and your peers with whom you established a network throughout your teacher preparation program. Isolation is the number one enemy of beginning teachers!

5. Understand that your enthusiasm can more than compensate for your lack of experience. Communicate to your new colleagues that you are willing to learn anything!

6. Relax and enjoy the first days with your students. Focusing on their needs will help you to avoid undue anxiety about your new, seemingly overwhelming responsibilities.

7. Recognize that you are serving in many capacities that you never thought possible. In the classroom, you quickly become a nurse, handyman, parent, counselor, referee, custodian, and entertainer.

8. Be patient with yourself!

9. Realize that many of the students deal with enormous family/social challenges. Particularly at the beginning of the school year, recognize that many of the students may be inexperienced or under-exposed rather than intellectually slow.

10. Understand that you will be compared to other teachers. Recognize that this is natural and, for the most part, without ill intent.

Interview conducted with
Virginia Villalovos, bilingual teacher.